Resilience Matters

Resilience Matters

A Memoir

Joanne Bellontine

authorHOUSE®

AuthorHouse™
1663 Liberty Drive
Bloomington, IN 47403
www.authorhouse.com
Phone: 1-800-839-8640

First published by AuthorHouse   11/16/2009

ISBN: 978-1-4490-4788-7 (e)
ISBN: 978-1-4490-4787-0 (sc)
ISBN: 978-1-4490-4786-3 (hc)

Library of Congress Control Number: 2009911821

Printed in the United States of America
Bloomington, Indiana

This book is printed on acid-free paper.

To my husband Joe, without whose love and suppot this would not have happened. To my family and friends, especially Nicki who have always been there for me. I love you all.

Preface

Joanne's story is extraordinarily compelling. She emerged from a life of abuse and neglect, to embody those all too elusive qualities: happiness, connection, perspective and purpose.

Her range of experience would fell lesser mortals, but, as you will read, Joanne manages to somehow maintain her integrity and sense of self throughout. None of this could be accomplished without a resilience I've rarely encountered in my work as a family therapist or my life in general.

Whether you're the product of a dysfunctional family, a foster child, a breast cancer survivor, or the victim of domestic violence, Joanne's story is bound to move you. Joanne describes, in her wonderfully direct and down to earth style, her journey through despair to a place of contentment. The feisty little girl who was so buffeted by life ultimately grew into a wise woman, a woman who truly found her voice. Today, Joanne surrounds herself with loving family and devoted friends. She's created the life she could only dream of as a child.

It is my privilege to introduce Joanne to you through this brief preface. Our 30-year friendship has been one of my life's great gifts.

Nicki Huebbe

Introduction

It is a beautiful summer day and I am holding my three-year-old granddaughter who just awoke from her nap. In this quiet moment, I find myself gazing out the door of the great room and into our backyard. I marvel at the beauty of the flowers. At the same moment I feel Katherine's warm breath on my neck and I am overwhelmed by feelings of utter contentment. I ask myself, "How did I get here?"

As I let my thoughts wander, they return to the time when I was Katherine's age. My life then was so radically different from the one she is living. She enjoys a privileged life. All my grandchildren do. They are blessed with parents who "get it", parents who understand when you choose to bring children into the world, it is your job to care for them lovingly, thoughtfully, consistently. I decided to write this book for my children and grandchildren. But, over time, when friends and family read my early drafts, many suggested that my book could help others. It is a raw depiction of my life but I decided to be as frank as possible in the hope it might be meaningful to others.

My challenges, setbacks and, successes, serve as an illustration of what life can become when you truly believe there's nothing you can't do if you keep trying and don't give up. It's a testament to the value of pulling up those proverbial bootstraps and believing in yourself and your dreams.

"Resilient Matters" is the story of my journey to a place of contentment and connection

One

We were on the school bus, on our way back to our suburban home in upstate New York, the place where my brother, sister and I had lived for the past year. In fact, this was the best of the series of foster homes we'd lived in. Grandma and Grandpa, our foster parents, tried to treat us as if we were one of their own. They had two grown children a son Richard, who had two daughters and a daughter Ada who had a daughter. Sadly, we always knew we would be different. But I didn't admit to being a foster child, not to my classmates or anyone. Instead, I made up outlandish stories about the mother who gave us away.

"She's a very important person." I told Katherine Hunt that day on the school bus. Katherine was homeroom monitor, also teacher's pet.

"She works for Tiffany's on Fifth Avenue." I went on. Katherine looked bewildered, as if she wasn't sure what was sold at Tiffany's

"That's the big jewelry store in New York City." I went on with real authority as if I'd recently shopped there. Of course I hadn't, but Katherine didn't know that. Like most women in my rural upstate New York neighborhood, her mother did not work or have a career like my fantasy mother.

"She flies all over the country on buying trips." I was on a roll. Katherine's eyes were wide with excitement. For a moment I think she wanted to have a mom like mine.

"Do you ever get to go with her?" Katherine asked.

"Oh no those trips are usually when we are in school so we can't go."

"That's why we live here in the country with Grandma." I slid back on the bus seat.

"Mama misses us terribly and wants us to live with her in New York, however she's away on business so often, and it just isn't possible." Katherine blinked but I was sure she believed me. Who could make up such an outrageous lie? Oh how I wished it were true! Oh if that could have been true, what a different life we might have had. It would have been wonderful to have an exciting, sophisticated, globe-trotting mother instead of the mother I had.

Before we were carted off to a series of foster homes, my family lived in an apartment over Gilinski's Bar and Grill and next to a Chinese laundry on New York City's lower east side. It was what they called a cold water flat, typical of the tenements in the 1940s. This was a place where you shared a bathroom in the hall with the other families living on the same floor. One of the teenagers upstairs, Michael McManus, whistled really loud, as he ran down the stairs rattling the doorknob on the bathroom door, spooking my sister and me while we were brushing our teeth. I was afraid he or someone else would barge in while we were in there, so I would be sure to pull the wooden stool over, stand on it and lock the door.

The door to our apartment opened into our small kitchen that had a big sink that doubled as our bathing area. The kitchen window looked out onto the fire escape and down to the alley below. There was a small closet in the kitchen, a stove and a small table with a couple of chairs, certainly not enough for all of us to share a meal, but we almost never ate together as a family anyway.

There were no bedrooms other than one that was kind of like a sleeper car on a train. It didn't have a door, but rather, a curtain to pull across. The living room was not very big, but it had two windows that looked down to the street below. One other small room off the living room was usually locked.

"You kids don't ever go in there. That's where Herman keeps his stuff" Mom would say with a stern face, wild-looking eyes and never a smile.

"What stuff?" I would ask. She would look at me with fire in her eyes and wag her finger in my face.

"You just don't ever go in there or you will be sorry you hear me young lady?"

"Yes mom, I hear you." I replied and she returned to washing some clothes in the kitchen sink.

I was just six years old, red headed, with a runny nose and dirty face always anxious. I walked in fear that something bad was going to happen and it usually did. I try to make sure I always know what is going on around me. A nervous little kid with no voice!

We kids slept on the cool brown and grey linoleum floor in the front room on blankets. We each had our designated spot. My sister Gerry's was closest to the wall and mine was to the right of hers. Ron and John's spots were under the front windows, so they could get up in the night and watch the action on the street below. Since our apartment was above the bar there was always some sort of commotion going on: an occasional street fight or a shouting match between a couple who had had too much to drink. If there was something really interesting, they would let us take a look otherwise it was out of bounds for us girls. Ron would, however, recount any arguments he witnessed, relishing the opportunity to use bad language! Here we were, four kids preparing to bed down for the night. What an unlikely group, four little kids all born to the same mother within six years of each other and each from a different father. Of course, we did not know that at the time. When we asked mom about our father, she would usually ignore us or change the subject. When pressed, she would give us a long cold stare and take a drag on her ever-present cigarette.

"He died in the war," she said once.

"Which war?" Ron would ask.

"The last one."

Somehow I never remember my mother being there, but when she was she was usually in the kitchen, standing by the sink with an apron on. She was a tall, thin woman with dark hair and was always very busy doing stuff what I don't know but she was busy, busy, and busy. She spent a lot of time telling us to be quiet and not to wake Herman, her boyfriend, who lived with us.

"After all, he pays the rent," she would say. I didn't know why that was so important but we were told that a lot. It was as if she were trying to sell us something.

"You know, Herman is very good to you kids," she said.

3

"He puts food on the table, pays the rent and puts up with all of you."

I never quite understood her definition of good. Was it good to tolerate us so he could have mom around? Was it good to beat the crap out of John and Ron every chance he had? Or maybe it was good of him to give us any food that was left over when he finished eating. I am not sure but she seemed to want us to like and respect him, even though he was anything but likeable or respectable.

Herman was a huge man, six foot plus barrel-chested with freckles all over his face. He had a thick crop of dark red hair and he wore black thick horn rimmed glasses. One day Ron was playing in the street when Herman was on his way home.

"Get upstairs," he ordered and Ron didn't move fast enough so I watched Herman kick and slap my brother all the way up the stairs. When they arrived in the apartment, mom said nothing. She just gave Herman a kiss hello and served dinner for the two of them. When they were done eating, we kids got to eat what was left. There was very little left but we made due we were use to that. I never remember mom smiling or laughing until Herman came home. Then she was a different person. That's when she became cheery and full of laughter. Herman loved her laugh. When he was not home, I remember her crying. I never really knew why but she was always sad and as I think back I don't think she was ever happy but she needed him.

Herman was the super which meant he cleaned, painted and fixed things around the building. Mom told us he was an architect by trade. I was pretty sure this was just another one of her stories. Even then I knew this was not the job an architect would have.

When she wasn't home, I guess my mother was working, trying her best to help support us kids. At least that's what we thought. I was always afraid when Mom was not there. There were men hanging around playing cards and drinking with Herman and that made me nervous. They would laugh and poke us when we would run past. Whenever we could we'd play in the street until mom came home or until the men left. I didn't know what they were drinking, but the stench would make my sister and me gag.

As the oldest girl, I felt compelled to care for my siblings. It was expected of me, a silent order I was given from my mother. I must have been about five when I first made lettuce and mayo sandwiches for my brothers and sister. But many times there was no bread, no lettuce, no mayo or anything for that matter. When that was the case I went to the store and went shopping. I would waltz into O'Reilly's Groceries, stroll down the dried goods aisle, shifting my gaze to the man at the register, while nonchalantly stuffing a can of peas under my coat. Next I might walk to another aisle for a box of pasta again slipping it under my coat and waltzing back towards the door. Since I had no money, I just took what I needed, hid the food under my clothes and rushed out of the store. One day the man at the register stopped me.

"What are you up to, cutie?" he asked.

"Oh nothing," I replied. I stiffened when he came towards me and my heart almost stopped beating, but he simply handed me a candy bar and patted me on the head.

"Get on home" he said. I ran all the way back to the apartment and shared that candy bar with Ron, John & Gerry. What a treat!

Stealing was a practice I resorted to when there was absolutely nothing in the apartment to eat. I had no other choice. I believe the storeowner knew exactly what I was doing and looked the other way. After all, it wasn't candy I was stealing. As a result, I learned very early on that you could exist without eating very much. Maybe that's why today I am such an accomplished dieter when I choose to be!

Hard to believe but our breakfast was often a slice of bread split four ways. When we finished we would head for the front room. Herman would be lying in the sleeper car bedroom, snoring, his genitals exposed, and the stench of liquor rising off him as we walked past to get to the front room. When we would complain to mom she said nothing and did nothing, not even cover him up or pull the curtain.

"After all, it is his money that helps buy the food," she said. One day I was so hungry that my belly ached and I ignored my mother's warnings about Herman eating first and helped myself to food meant for him. When she realized what I had done she grabbed me by the hair, kicked me behind my knees and made me kneel on a handful of split peas for the rest of the day. Kneeling on split peas was my mother's punishment of choice. When Herman got up he decided I should scrub the entire kitchen floor with a toothbrush. I did that scrubbing until he left for work then mom let me stop. My knees were so sore and my hands ached from holding that tooth brush for such a long time.

"Well young lady I hope you have learned your lesson?" she said.

"Yes mom I have." I was sent to my place on the floor for the rest of the night without supper. My stomach noises supplied music for my brothers and sister until they fell asleep. No one really cared or had the capacity to care about us. Certainly not my mother or Herman.

When I consider it now, the daily stress we were forced to endure is unimaginable. I cringe when I think of my children and grandchildren enduring what we went through. The hardest punishment I've ever handed out was taking away a favorite toy (for a while) or giving a time out. If nothing else my harsh treatment as a child certainly shaped my behavior as an adult and a parent. I wouldn't treat an animal the way we were treated as children.

But at the time, I thought everyone lived like us. When you entered the building where we lived, you could smell the urine and beer in the hallway. The stairs were dimly lit and filthy. Once you got into our apartment it was cold, dank and mostly empty. I remember being confused about so many things that went on in that apartment. I have a faint memory of going for a walk with my mother and ending up at some kind of clinic. I was not sure what we were doing there, but I do remember seeing wall charts depicting babies in the womb. Of course, I did not know at the time that it was a womb! On our walk home, mom cried a lot. Only later did I find out that at the clinic mom had learned she was pregnant. Apparently, she dreaded telling Herman that she was going to have another baby. This would be the first of two daughters she would have with him.

When we got back to the apartment, Herman was a sleep. Mom just sat in a chair in the kitchen wringing her hands. She seemed very nervous and looked sad. When he woke up she broke the news.

"Well guess what? You're going to be a father." Herman looked over at her.

"You better be kidding," his voice got loud. My mother hung her head.

"Dam it," he screamed walking towards her.

"Tell me you are kidding!"

That's when my sister and I ran to the front room and hid under the table. Mom said nothing. We watched Herman slap her, and then watched as she ran into the kitchen with him right behind her. He was screaming obscenities and slapping at her all over.

"Herman, please stop," she cried. But he did not stop.

"You stupid bitch, how could you let this happen!" His face was beat red and he was flailing his arms around and then pounded the kitchen table so hard I thought it would split in half.

"The last thing we need around here is another mouth to feed." He picked up one of my mother's high heels, which had fallen off in her attempt to get away. He hit her on the head with it. Blood was running down her face. My sister and I, while hiding under the table, were thinking we might be next.

Suddenly he stopped, panting, out of breath. He wiped his mouth.

"Going to Gilinski's." He turned towards the door, looked back at her sitting there on the floor bleeding.

"You stupid bitch!" he screamed before walking out the door.

Gerry and I ran to the kitchen and tried to help.

"Mom, are you okay?" We knew she was not okay, but we asked.

"I'll be fine." She was on the floor, shaking and crying. She suddenly collected herself.

"Get me a towel and wet it." I pulled the stool over to reach the sink, wet the cloth and gave it to her. She began cleaning the blood off her face.

"Someday you will understand," she said, about Herman.

"You are too young for me to explain this to you now." Mom tied a scarf on her head and the three of us walked to the hospital to see about mom's head. Once there, they took her right in because she was bleeding. The nurse in the emergency room clicked her pen on mom's chart.

"So what happened?" she asked. Mom's voice sounded high and unfamiliar.

"Oh I was working in the kitchen and a heavy pot fell off the shelf and the handle hit my head." I started to say something but mom got that fire in her eyes look and I said nothing. I don't know if they believed her, but they asked no further questions. They put a few stitches in her head and the three of us went home.

My mother was a battered woman, I would learn later, as I would later become. Remarkably after the incident, everything went back to normal, and Herman, now over his tantrum, was as sweet as pie. He was giving hugs and kisses all around, just like one big happy family. John & Ron came home and asked what had happened. I think for the first time in my young life I truly realized that not only was my life crazy so was everyone around me. I also knew silence was golden.

"What happened?" my brothers asked and she told them the same story she told the nurses at the hospital, which seemed to satisfy them. We were easily satisfied as children.

"Yea," Herman chimed in.

"We gotta get a better way to stack those pots." Mom probably thought if she told the boys the truth that they would confront Herman. Ron had a very short fuse, which meant he would try to defend his mother. This would ultimately earn him a beating from Herman. As I look back I realize I was negatively affected in many ways. Even today, I am always looking over my shoulder. I fear unfamiliar things and I am generally not quick to respond or react to new things. All these years later, I'm still that anxious kid in some ways.

Years later, after Herman moved out, Ron often told the story of how he thought he saw Herman on a bus and how he chased that bus for many blocks.

"I hate that bastard so much" Ron told me.

"I would have killed him if I ever saw him again," he said and I believed him.

Even as a child, I realized how truly amazing it was that one day my mother could be sent to the hospital with a head injury and wake up the next morning, acting as if nothing had happened. It was as if she'd not been stitched up the night before, but was simply carrying on business as usual. She was the one who got up first. Then we were up folding our blankets, stacking them on the floor near our spots. All the while Herman slept like a baby in the sleeper car down the hall, making all kinds of nasty noises as he slept.

It was my job to take the empty milk bottles back to the store for deposit. My sister Gerry had gone down the stairs before me. As I stood on the landing gathering the milk bottles, I heard sounds coming from the stairs below. I stood watching a man standing over my sister, pressing her body against the dirty plaster wall. A bare bulb burned dimly above them. The bottles shifted in the bag.

"What the …." The man turned and looked up, squinting in the dimly lit hallway. I heard Gerry's voice.

"Joanne!" Her hand stretched out to me, her jacket open, blouse torn.

All I could think about was the fever she had had that kept her sleeping and listless, on the floor for three days. Automatically, as if I'd been doing it my whole life I lobbed a milk bottle straight at the man's head. I saw the surprise in his eyes before he ducked. Glass crashed on the wall.

"Get out" I heard myself growl.

I did not know what else to do but knew I had to do *something*, so I just reacted and threw the rest of the milk bottles, down the stairs, one after another. The man ran away. I was very pleased with myself and, of course, my sister was too. We ran back upstairs to our apartment and I proudly recounted my accomplishment.

"Did you break all the damn bottles?" My mother then demanded. She was angry because I had broken the bottles which meant no deposit, I couldn't believe it! My punishment was the usual, kneeling on split peas with my face to the wall for a very long time. I wonder where Mom got the money for those split peas. I have often thought in my adult years, for God's sake, did she not realize I had saved Gerry from being molested? Was the deposit for the bottles worth more than her own daughter's body? I think at the time, the deposit was more valuable to my mom. I didn't care how long I had to kneel on those peas; it was worth every minute. As I knelt, I cried and tried to understand what I had done wrong. Some of those pea kneeling sessions lasted for hours. I would think bad thoughts about my mom, like maybe she would fall down and scrape her knees then maybe she would understand how mean this punishment was. But the longer I knelt the sadder I got. Maybe I really was a bad kid and deserved this punishment. Most of all, with every split pea kneeling session, I became angrier and angrier at mother. I'd like her less and less. I sometimes wished I could run away and never see her or the apartment again. I would soon learn to be careful what I wished for!

While our beds consisted of a spot on the floor, our night-light was a Miller High Life beer sign that hung on the wall of the front room like a piece of fine art. It filled up a beer glass and then emptied it. We did okay, my sister and brothers we were just like most other kids, or so I thought. We still occasionally had fun. Ron and John played the usual big brother tricks on us. I remember one day John ran to the street and called up to the front room window to Gerry and me. We ran to the window with great anticipation only to find my brother John on the street hoisting water balloons up to the fire escape. Gerry walked onto the fire escape and John lobed a balloon and got her right in the face. I ran to see what the commotion was all about and I got slammed on my head. I was so angry I ran downstairs but John was nowhere in sight. Ron, on the other hand, got us in different ways. Very often he would watch for us to go to the bathroom for our morning wash up. Once in the bathroom he would wedge the door and we would be left screaming and yelling for someone to let us out. Ron would leave for the day to play with friends. Sometimes it might be a while till we were freed but most times it was just a few minutes. I spent many hours trying to figure out what to do to get him back, but I never did. All in all it was an okay life for us, or so we thought.

When my brothers weren't tormenting their sisters, they were out in the street playing with other kids. Many times when my mom was home, she told us to stay outside and play.

"Only come in when you are called!" she'd say. I often wondered why we were not allowed to come back to the apartment. Now I know it was better not to know what was going on inside.

During our childhood, Gerry and I were inseparable and would be for many years. The birth of my two little sisters Pauline and then Jamie would belong to a time marked by certain life-changing events. Pauline was born after the fire, an incident that would alter our lives forever. Jamie would be born after we were taken away from our mother for good. But I'm getting ahead of myself.

All in all, I would say the boys had it tougher than we girls, or so it seemed. I remember playing cops and robbers with Ron and John. Of course, I was the robber; I don't know why but the boys always determined who played what roles. We all armed ourselves with weapons for the game. Gerry and I decided our plan of attack. The boys tried to intimidate us, as older brothers do, letting us know they were in charge and would ultimately conquer us in battle. Well, as the game intensified and the pace heightened, I ran out on the fire escape to hide from my brothers, the cops. They thought they were so tough, I was certain that Gerry and I would be the winners. Then I heard one of them coming out on the fire escape: it was Ron and I bolted. My weapon, the broom, was in place and I was ready to conquer the evil villain. Unfortunately, as I positioned myself to shoot, Ron leapt out the window onto the fire escape. There was nowhere to run to, and as I was quite small, I fell through the railing to the ground one flight below. When I think of that terrible incident, I realize I was lucky. I didn't die or become crippled for life. I just fell and broke my back.

The next thing I remember was lots of people around me as I lay on the ground. Some of them strapped me to a board and put me on a stretcher and then lifted me into the ambulance. I heard the sound of the siren blaring and there was lots of fussing over me. The people in the ambulance put needles in my arm and a mask over my mouth and told me to breathe normally.

"I want my mother!" I said though I wasn't quite sure what she would do.

"She'll meet us at the hospital," a medic said. When we arrived, the ambulance doors flew open and nurses came in to check me before they took me inside where everything was cold and white and I was in a bed. A bed! I had never been in a bed before. My body ached and I didn't see anyone familiar. Where was my mom, my siblings? Where was anyone I knew?

"You're in a hospital honey," a nurse said. What was that? I remember a clean room where everything was white, the floors, and the uniforms of the women who changed my nightgown. I got a clean hospital gown every day that smelled of bleach. The nurse said I could keep it even when I went home. She asked if I was cold every time she came into the room.

"No" I said. My back had been broken and I had some internal injuries. I was in pain, but I was impressed with the really warm and comfy bed I was in and the sheets were so clean and fresh smelling. Somehow, I do remember it was not so bad. At least, not for me. I had a bed to sleep in, three meals a day, and clean, fresh clothes to wear. As if that were not enough, there were people who seemed to genuinely care about me. They took time to read me a bedtime story before tucking me in. What was not to like? I will say, I did feel guilty about not being home for Gerry but I think between the pain and the medication I didn't really care. I was very upset that my mom did not come to the hospital. The nurses told me that she had called but needed to stay home to care for the other children. I was confused about this, but I ultimately gave her a get out of jail card because she was doing my job. Oh well, I must admit I really did not care I was having a great time with these people. All new sensations for me, which were nice. I really don't remember how long I was in the hospital but it was a long time. When I did get out of bed the nurses let me help them fold towels and wash clothes. Then they would tell me stories and fix my hair. One day one of the nurses came to spend time with me and gave me ribbons for my hair. She told me I looked like a princess! No one had ever told me anything like that.

In time to come, mom would blame Ron for the accident. Like the rest of us, Ron had no voice and did not protest. Young as I was, I knew it was not his fault. Ron was often blamed for everything, even the fire that would disrupt our lives forever.

The fire. I was seven and we were still living above Gilinski's Bar, next to the Chinese laundry. Gerry and I were sick with fevers and coughed a lot. It may have been pneumonia. We just lay there, being sick.

Suddenly, I looked into the kitchen area and could see smoke. The walls seemed to be painted in gray and big puffs of smoke filled our apartment the smoke was coming from the kitchen. Our apartment was on fire. Gerry rolled over and looked at me with her make it better look. But this was one order I could not fill. We clutched at each other hoping to make it go away. We were too sick to move. Weak from fever and so, so scared we watched the room fill with smoke. Then it happened, we saw our first flames and knew we were in big trouble. Gerry began to cry and I joined her when suddenly a couple of firemen broke the door down.

"You get the other one," one of them said as he scooped me up in his arms. The men carried us down stairs and left us next door at the laundry.

There was a lot of yelling and water was being sprayed up into the air at the apartment building. One of the firemen asked how many people were in our apartment. I told him it was just Gerry, Ron and me, but Ron left. I did not know where everyone else was. While the fireman talked, the laundry workers gave Gerry and me cookies and milk.

With great commotion, the firemen went in and out of the apartment and finally succeeded in putting out the fire.

I remember looking at the charred building and watching water run down the front and the smell of smoke and burned paint filled the air. I wasn't sure just what to do so I stood up and turned to my sister.

"That's it." I told my sister.

"We can go back now." It seemed simple. I thought that was all that had to be done and we would go back to our apartment. Everything would go back to normal however, that was not to be. We sat there, in the laundry, with people asking questions and wondering about mom. Where is she? It was as if the world was moving around us in swirls. We watched as people around us were running up and down the stairs from the laundry to the apartment. Water was everywhere, running down the stairs and out into the street. People on the street stopped and stared at the building. As Gerry and I sat in the Chinese laundry the smell of food came trailing into the room we were in and it smelled warm and yummy. I remember thinking boy wouldn't it be good to have some of that to eat!

A short time later, some ladies, social workers, I think, arrived and began to ask us a lot of questions. They seemed kind, as if they really cared about us.

"Where is your Mom?" one of them asked

"I don't know" I said as innocently as I could. I really didn't know where mom was. All I knew is that she left early that morning with our brother John. I was pretty sure she was going to that place that had those pictures of babies on the wall. It was very hard to know what to say I was afraid if I said too much I would get a little more than the fire-in-her-eyes look from mom.

"How many of you live in this apartment?" One woman fingered a button on her coat.

"Me, my sister and two brothers," I said. Then worrying about my life, I told her the rest.

"And mom and her friend Herman." I hoped I had not said too much: the ladies seemed very serious. Only as I grew older did I realize that I had added another red flag to the story. Not only did my mother leave two small children alone. She was living with Herman and they were not married. In the 1940's this was not the norm. The woman took down what I said, and when they were finished told us that we needed to go with them.

"Where are we going?" my sister asked me.

"I don't know," I replied. Somehow I knew our lives would be irrevocably changed. I don't know how I knew but I did. My heart was beating very fast and I thought it would burst through my chest. Then I looked over at Gerry who had that *'make it better Joanne'* look which I'd seen so many times. I was pretty sure this time I could not do that.

"Where the hell is Mom?" I blurted out looking up and down the street. Gerry and I had been asleep when she left that morning. I had no clue where she might be, though, I was pretty sure she would return she always came back.

Years later I would learn I was right. My mother had been at the clinic for a pregnancy check-up. We usually did not know where mom went when she was not at the apartment. We thought she was working but this time because she took John with her I knew she was not working.

Just as we were getting ready to leave with the social workers, mom came running up stairs only to be turned back by the remaining firemen.

"Are you're looking for the two little girls?"

"Yes I am, where the hell are my girls?"

"We took them to the laundry downstairs." She turned and ran back down the stairs and into the laundry.

"What the hell is going on here?" My mother demanded to know. Only my mother would adopt such a tone in circumstances like these. John was with her, his eyes darting all around. He looked over at me with a look of what the heck is going on here!

"You get out of here and leave my kids alone," mom yelled at the social workers. One of them stepped forward and glared at my mother.

"Well Mrs. Jackson, we cannot do that, you see these children were left unattended and could have died in this fire."

My mother sized her up.

"You are exaggerating" she protested.

"Just leave and I will make it all better." She was rubbing her face and breathing very heavy, pacing back and forth.

"I'm afraid we can't do that," the social worker said. I heard an ambulance in the distance. This was not going to end well, I somehow knew.

"Joanne, where is Ron?" My mother asked. I looked down at the ground.

"I don't know."

"Perhaps he ran out of the apartment when he thought he heard someone coming up the stairs," I offered. If you wanted to hide from someone, you would hide in the hall and go down the stairs when they went into the apartment. But then I realized that it was right after he left that smoke started to fill the kitchen. Mom tried to go into the apartment but the firemen would not let her.

"What do you mean?" I heard her say. I watched the whole scene, my mother arguing with the fireman, with the social worker.

I had so many questions. Where were we going to live? Where would we sleep that night? Did the Miller high life beer sign burn in the fire?" All I could see was the glare from the street signs and the only light was coming from Gilinsky's. I looked to mom for answers, but none came. Now she was crying. The social workers were saying something to her and she was crying hard. Then without any further talk, the social worker opened the door to her car and I got in. It was as if I were in a trance. The social worker walked around the car and opened the other door and Gerry and John got in. We spoke not a word. I looked back and mom was just standing there all alone. I must say I did feel sorry for her and scared for us. We had no idea what lie ahead for us. The engine started and we drove off. I turned and waved out the window but mom was gone.

Oh my God, where are they taking us? Why is mom not coming with us, she can't sleep in the apartment either. Gerry, John and I were not understanding, why mom didn't come with us after all, if we couldn't go back into the apartment, neither could she. I decided she was going to find Ron and then join us. That's what I thought when we took off in the car. Somehow, that made me feel better.

But that never happened and a few months later, when Pauline was born, Pauline would join John in one placement center, while Gerry and I were sent to a different one. Life, as we knew it, had ended for our family. The future was just a foggy picture. The Jackson kids had just been shot into space and where they would land would be anyone's guess.

Over the next few months there was a lot of talk about how the fire started. The prevailing thought was that my brother Ron had been playing with matches. As a result, Ron was taken away, seemingly forever. We did not see him; we never knew where he went or how he was doing. My world was out of control. I tried to picture him in my head so I would not forget what he looked like. I wanted a photograph but there were no pictures. I was so afraid he was gone forever. I asked anyone who would listen for information about my brother but no one could or would answer that question.

We would later learn that he was placed in Bellevue Psychiatric Hospital, then in a series of foster homes, and ultimately in a facility in Kings Park Hospital. They were going to fix him, reform him. Surely, any boy who could start a fire and then run away leaving two sick sisters asleep in the front room was mentally ill. It was truly a tragic day for us but more so for Ron, because all of these places were dreadful. The misreading of the situation, along with cruelty, negligence, and abuse that he (and other children) suffered, would have a strong impact on my brother for his entire life. Ron was at Kings Park a year before he ran away and went back to the apartment. He would later say that he was happy he remembered the way. He ran up the stairs and pounded on the door. Our mother answered the door and shushed him before she stepped out into the hallway. I imagine her standing there, tall and frail with a cigarette in one hand. As Ron begins to speak she takes a drag on the cigarette.

"Please, please can I come back home?" Ron would later say.

"I promise I will be good, really good mom, I promise." He dropped to his knees and held onto her dress. Imagine my mother staring at him, deciding how she would break the news.

"They are really mean to me at Kings Park and some of the adults do nasty things to me." He began to cry and clung to mom. Knowing her, she probably stood there looking down at him. She was a woman of little emotion, who knew how to take care of herself.

"I'm sorry Ron, Herman pays the rent and does not want kids around" she would finally say. Distraught, and with no place else to go Ron returned to the facility where he stayed until he was about fifteen. Then he ran away for good and lived a difficult life which he doesn't talk about much.

Many years later, before he married, Ron would locate Gerry and me. He knew he had sisters and confided to me that he was always afraid he would accidently marry one of us. Well Ron did not marry his sister and when he married his first wife, Jean, we attended the wedding. Gerry and I were then 16 and 17.

But that was after the fire, long after. After a series of foster homes, our separation and eventual reunion. I don't remember much about the apartment where the fire took place. Like our brother Ron, who was not invited into our mother's apartment, we were never invited back to see. But I do recall a lot of smoke and a nasty smell hanging in the air. When the dust settled and the day came to an end, we were brought to a place called a children's shelter. Of course, we did not know what that was. We were taken away and did not see our mother until months later.

Gerry and I were installed in a temporary children's shelter in Manhattan, where we stayed until we were eventually placed into foster care by Leake and Watts Children's Home. The shelter offered a rather utilitarian environment in which we were fed, given baths and put to bed the bare minimum level of care; however, it was far more than we were accustomed to. We and all the other children were in a cavernous room with white walls and rows and rows of white metal beds with head and side railings on them. I was glad to see the rails because I was afraid if I rolled over I would fall out. That had not been a problem when sleeping on the floor. As difficult as the experience was, sleeping in a bed was novel for me. Except for my experience in the hospital, I had always slept on the floor and that was what I knew. When I climbed up into that bed it was awesome. I loved it and felt a little guilty about that. I wondered where my brothers' would be sleeping and if Gerry would be okay sleeping across the room. I remember how scared I was, tears running down my face trying to locate my sister in the crowded room of beds.

For the first time in our lives, Gerry and I were separated. Although I am sure there was some perverse psychological or administrative reason for it. Gerry was only four years old, tiny and frightened, and she needed me. That night as I tried to sleep, sleep would not come. All I heard were Gerry's whimpers coming from the back of the cavernous room. I got out of my bed and made my way back to hers. I crawled along the floor occasionally bumping into other kid's beds, until I crawled my way to her.

"Are you okay?" I whispered to her.

"My nose," she said, crying harder. In addition to being frightened and sad, she was having a nosebleed. I crawled back to the bathroom and got two cold wet washcloths to put on her head and the back of her neck. She had had nosebleeds before and I knew this would work. I changed the washcloth several times, each time making the crawl to the front of the room and then to the bathroom.

"Everything will be okay." I tried to sound as reassuring as possible though I wasn't at all sure anything would be right again. Her whimpering and tears finally stopped and she fell asleep. I worked my way back to my bed, but because of the many trips all night my nightgown was quite soiled. I just got settled, closed my eyes, when someone came in and threw on the lights.

"Up and at it," the floor monitor said. Wow I was tired. No one knew that I had been up most of the night with my sister. I don't think they would have cared if they did know. The temporary children's shelter was a place that simply had the responsibility to bed down children for the night, get us up, washed, fed and off to school.

School! I had no idea what that was. I must have been about seven but I had never been to school. That night we arrived we were told the clothes we were wearing were all we would have. Each night when we would wash for bed, we would also have to wash and wring out our panties and socks, then hang them over the bed railing to dry. How could a child so young understand how to do this? Of course, the underwear was still wet in the morning. As I thought of putting on wet clothing, I tearfully complained to the woman in charge.

"Well, I guess tonight you will do a better job," she told me. I think of my grandchildren at this age, washing and wringing out their underwear and socks and I can't get my brain around that thought. I know they are more privileged than I was but no way is a child that age capable of doing an okay job with this task. I got used to wearing damp panties and socks!

I attended my first day of school, which was in the same building where we were living, down the hall from the cafeteria. Despite the wet underwear, I was full of wonder and excitement. I was very impressed with the other children. They could read and some of them could even write. I had no idea what that was all about however I embraced the idea of learning.

Gerry and I shared a desk, but that's as far as my memory goes. This may be because my eyesight was so bad that it was so hard for me to take in information. I would later be told that my vision was so poor as a child that I was considered legally blind. I was just born with very bad eyesight, although I am sure that our poor diet exacerbated the condition. Only at age nine, when I was finally placed in a permanent foster home, was this problem addressed and I was fitted up for my first pair of glasses.

"It was amazing; I didn't know I had green eyes!" I was also surprised to know just how red and shiny my hair could be with proper shampoo: it had always looked dull and fuzzy before. With my new spectacles, everything seemed to come to life and it was as if someone had washed the world.

Day after day, Gerry and I did what we were told. Everyone had chores like dusting the furniture. Some of the older girls would set the tables in the cafeteria others cleaned up when we were done. Since Gerry and I were younger, we just dusted and folded laundry. And we patiently waited for our mother to come and get us. But that didn't happen. She never came.

When we were first placed in the children's shelter she came to visit one day but never returned. I remember that day very clearly. Mom came bouncing into the visiting room arms laden with gifts. She was dressed in a long winter coat, her hair wavy and pretty. As she strolled across the room packages were falling onto the floor and we scrambled to her to pick them up.

"Mom have you come to take us home?"

"No girls they won't let me."

"They tell me I have a disease that you kids could catch so we need to be apart a little longer."

"How long?" I asked.

"I can't say right now, they don't seem to know." As happy as we were to see her she was not telling us what we wanted to hear. All she wanted to talk about was the stuff she brought and would not answer any questions we had about going home. I got very angry and she knew it, she tried to hug me and I pulled away. The visit soon ended she said she had to go to work. As I look back, years later I wonder if she would have come back to visit if we had been more pleasant. Five and seven year old children don't have much tact.

One day as we were doing our usual waiting, a lady came into our classroom and asked our teacher to get our things together. Maybe we are going home, mom said she had been trying and trying to find another apartment and now we could go home. I was sure of that. But at first I was hopeful and told Gerry.

"I bet mom is here and going to take us home," I said. I had known the ropes and rules at home here they were all very strange and confusing to me. Wow, we really thought we were going home. Maybe Ron and John would be there and we could all be together again. Maybe mom will be a better mother. Maybe she'd gotten rid of Herman. I was willing to give her another chance. When I found out that mom was not there for us, it was as if someone had punched me in the stomach. What we did not know was we were on our way to what would be the first of several foster homes.

The words foster home I find difficult to digest, even now. I knew early on that when I became a foster child as a person, I did not matter and neither did my opinion. At least at home I was in charge of Gerry and knew how to take care of her. At the foster home, no one ever asked how they should care for her or how I was feeling about anything. If perhaps I was brave enough to voice an opinion, I was very quickly told to keep quiet. Any questions I dared to ask were never answered. It really wasn't much different from home except in a foster home we ate three squares a day and had a bed to sleep in. We were told these people were there to help us and make our lives better.

"Where is our Mom?" I would ask.

"When are we going home?

"Why are we here?" My questions were endless. No one seemed to think it mattered if we knew anything about the direction of our lives. At least at home we knew what to expect day-to-day. It was familiar and we had learned how to survive in that environment. Once, though, someone patted me on the head and told me to hang in there. At that moment a pat on the head was about as much caring and sensitivity as I could have hoped for.

So our journey through the foster care system had begun. One foster home was in New Jersey, an uncomfortable place, both emotionally and physically. Our foster *parents*, if you can call them that, treated us as if we had no feelings. We were never asked if we wanted to do anything. We were always told what to do. We might as well be back in our old apartment. At least there we did what we wanted! Somehow at the ripe old age of eight, I felt I had lost my independence. You have to remember we were street kids and pretty much on our own. This was all new to us. One day our new foster father, Jack told us he would be taking us for a boat trip. I expressed my objections and my propensity for motion sickness.

"Be ready at 6 a.m." He replied.

Really, no kid wants to go anywhere at 6 a.m. But he didn't seem to care. I had little experience with the outside world and its inhabitants. We were often told to just do as we are told and we would do just fine in this system. It was a system of rules and our job was to follow them.

So we did. Some folks took kids in because they liked them and wanted to help. And there were those who took in foster kids only to make money. And although many did it because they genuinely wanted to help, some didn't know how to treat small, scared children.

Jack was not someone who really wanted to help.

"Is Rose coming?" I asked Jack about the boat trip. Rose was his wife, our new foster mother.

"No" he replied. It was very early in the morning, still a bit dark out; as we drove to the boat dock not a word was spoken. Gerry and I just sat holding each other's hands. We arrived and there was no one there, just lots of boats tied up waiting their turn to go for a ride. The air smelled of dampness and I tasted salt, the mist washed our faces.

We piled out of the car and I immediately stiffened. It was just him and us; I again asked why Rose was not coming. I got no reply. I didn't think much about it at that moment, however as I drift back in time to that moment, I felt very uncomfortable. I now wonder what he was thinking, taking two young, insecure girls out to sea. As the boat slowly drifted further and further from shore, my body got stiffer and stiffer. The water was so smooth, like a piece of shiny glass, not a sound except for the birds singing their early morning melodies. By the time the boat stopped, and the anchor was dropped, you could hardly see land. Gerry and I were in the back and Jack was driving the boat.

"Do we have to stay out here?" Gerry asked.

"I hope not" I said.

"I'll try to get Jack to take us back." He was at the helm and seemed happy. The water was calm and quite beautiful however the feeling was ominous. There were no other boats in sight, I wanted to scream at the top of my lungs, but there was no one to hear me. Jack would hit the throttle and make the boat go very fast then slow it down.

"You see that I can make this boat do anything I want it to." We sat there looking at Jack trying to figure out what was happening.

He hollered back at us.

"Get ready girls, we are going to have fun." We clung to the side of the boat so tightly; I think we peeled off the paint in our hands. Gerry was getting really upset and I could hardly breathe. I called out to him.

"I think I am going to throw up," I said.

"Don't worry, you will be fine," he said.

"The water is very calm. Remember you only get seasick if the water is rough."

"Please take us back to the house." I begged. Jack slowly made his way to the back of the boat and sat between Gerry and me. He slowly began to rub our backs. He then began to tell us how much fun we were going to have and once I got my sea legs I would feel better. I looked at Gerry and could see that look *Joanne make it better* look in her eyes. Jack proceeded to busy himself about the boat, I guess giving us time to get our sea legs whatever that meant. It wasn't happening and I went into survival mode. I began to cry then Gerry joined in. Now there was lots of noise coming from the back of that boat. Jack came to the back of the boat to calm us down but he could not. He was losing patience and pointed his finger at us.

"That's the trouble with you kind of kids," he said.

"I try to do something nice and you screw it up." Jack stomped to the front of the boat, pulled up the anchor and started the engine. He turned the boat around and headed for shore. I looked over at Gerry. Mission accomplished!

I have often relived that boat ride over in my mind and wondered what might have happened if I had not insisted we turn around. Maybe nothing, but I don't believe that. Not only was it inappropriate for this man to scare us it was way too soon to take two vulnerable girls out in a boat with just him. I still get chills when I relive that trip and will always believe my instincts were right.

I knew I wanted out of this house and to ensure that we would be booted out I suggested to Gerry that she wet the bed. In the children's shelter, if you wet the bed, you were seriously reprimanded. Sometimes a child might even be made to sleep in the wet sheets, just to teach them a lesson. I was sure this would do the trick. If it had not worked we would have to figure out another way to get sent back. I just knew this was not a safe place. I can't explain why but I knew we needed to get out of there.

It worked and in the morning when we got up our foster mother told us to strip the beds and take our stuff and put it in the paper bags she supplied. She seemed more angry than sad; she was losing her two new foster daughters. She walked up and down the hall until we had gathered our stuff and put it in the bags. When we were done she snatched the bags from our hands.

"Go eat and then get outside and wait for your pick up."

"Why?" I asked.

"Where are we going?" I asked naively, I played my part

"Back where you belong" she said.

That morning the social worker showed up and we were packed and on our way back to the children's shelter. The place where there was truly no joy or fun. It was like being in a prison. There were just rules, rules and more rules. If you broke a rule, you were paddled and sent to bed for the rest of the day with no meals. I must say although harsh not nearly as dreadful as kneeling on those split peas. Being treated badly was something we had gotten accustomed to and, like it or not, it was a part of our life. I saw my job of deciding between the children's shelter and this awful foster home as figuring out the lesser of two evils. At the children's shelter, we were never allowed outside, except on Saturday when each child was given ten cents and we walked to the corner candy store to buy candy. I must admit that was the highlight of our week! As dreadful as it was, it was known territory. So back we went. I was very pleased with myself and very happy that my sister could wet the bed on command. What a team. We were good at surviving.

We stayed at the children's shelter until the next foster family became available. These were couples who pledged to open their homes and hearts and treat us as if we were part of their family. Hah! There was one, then another, most of them bad to terrible experiences. In some of the foster homes we weren't even allowed to eat with the family or play with their children.

"You are here to work, not to play," one foster mother said, mercenary that she was. Being in a foster home was yet another new experience to which we'd learn to adapt. This scenario was repeated again and again until February 1952 when Gerry and I seven and nine respectively, were driven to a foster home in upstate New York. This environment was so different from the previous one somewhere in the city that I was sure we were in another country altogether. On the ride to our new home the landscape seemed more and more remote: no buildings, just lots and lots of fields and there were even animals in those fields with big sacks hanging down under their bellies. We would later learn that these were cows. We had never seen such sights. There were no tall buildings, no bus stops and very few cars. This was the beginning of our new life on Ludingtonville Road in Holmes, New York. The house looked like it was in the woods and there were lots of trees in front of it. As we got out of the car, a wild animal appeared and jumped on me. I was sure I was being attacked and would die. How was I supposed to know that this was a domestic pet called a dog?

Bimbo, the household pet, was really a sweet creature. However, I had never seen a dog, and I did not know he was only greeting me with dog kisses. I would later learn to love Bimbo and spend many hours romping with him. But for the moment, I was terrified but grateful to be alive. Then, standing behind the dog was a huge woman. I was bewildered by her size. Did this mean she was sick? Filled with helium like a balloon? But she seemed like a nice lady.

"Hello girls." She bent down, opened her arms and hugged us.

"Nice to meet you." She smiled and told us that we were going to have our own room and that we would sleep in the same bed. She tried to make us feel comfortable and she succeeded. Unlike our previous foster homes this one seemed different. There were family pets and not just Bimbo the dog. There was also a cat named Blackie. He was all black and even had black eyes. Blackie would become my pal. Blackie would ultimately sleep with Gerry and me! Our feelings about this place were that it would be okay.

In my mind's eye I see the house huge, with a large front porch, a spacious kitchen, living room and dining room. It was in fact like a mansion you would see in a magazine. There were even curtains on the windows and a tablecloth on the table in the kitchen, and enough chairs for everyone. In the dining room there was a lace tablecloth on the table the kind that rich people had. It was truly a magnificent place. There was a staircase, which led to four bedrooms and there was a bathroom and walk-in closet. This was so much space compared to the apartment we had lived in! Outside there was a big yard and plenty of room for flower gardens and a spot for a vegetable garden. Up back at the edge of the woods there was an outhouse, which we would learn all about when the weather got warmer and the well went dry.

For the next ten years this would be our home and during those years, we would have our ups and downs but at least we would be safe. One may not understand how important safe is, but had you lived in our world, you would understand the relief of having the chance to live a predictable life. Here we had routine and if you followed the rules and did as you were told, you knew you would not be beaten. *I, for one, was really happy to know that our foster mother had no split peas!* To have stability from day to day made us feel safe. Until now, life had been precarious and unpredictable. But now we had landed in a place where we had our own room, pets to love, adults who we thought would not beat us. Our life was all about rules and control. We followed the rules and they had control. You had to do something really bad in their minds to get a beating with grandpa's razor strap. It was important that you did your chores and not talk back, homework was a priority and life was as good as it could be. After three months we had a huge surprise our brother John and baby sister Pauline came to live with us! The fire incident had separated us; John was sent to a different children's shelter in the city. When Pauline was born she was placed in the same children's shelter with John. By now John was 11 and Pauline would be three that May. This would be the first time Gerry and I would be meeting Pauline since she was born after we were placed in the foster care system.

That day, the social worker, Mrs. Frazier, drove up the long driveway and out of the car bounded John and Pauline. What a cutie she was, a perfect looking child with beautiful curly blond hair. John looked like he had grown so tall and appeared much older than I remembered. Pauline was very chatty and a bit standoffish to grandma. She ran to Gerry and wanted to be picked up. Gerry picked her up and twirled her around she was laughing and I am sure not knowing this was her new home. John just stood there his head down and not looking comfortable.

"Where is mom? Is she coming?" I asked Mrs. Frazier.

"We will talk about your mom later." We never did. We were ecstatic to be reunited with John and very happy to meet our new baby sister Pauline. John was quiet and didn't say much. Pauline, however, was running around and rolling on the lawn. I asked if I could pick her up and when I did I felt like I had another child to care for. I carried her around most of the afternoon until grandma insisted on a turn. Gerry took the opportunity to show John first the yard then the house. She showed him our room and he was surprised to see we had our own room.

"Am I going to have my own room too?" John asked.

"I think so." Gerry pointed the way.

"The room right at the top of the stairs," Gerry responded. With the arrival of our two siblings, the tone of life changed immediately. Suddenly, there was lots of laughter, running, yelling and fun. I can't remember when we'd ever had pure fun before. But even better than having fun, was seeing that we might actually settle into a somewhat *normal* day-to-day life. I was truly thinking that this was the beginning of a real life for us. We would attend school, do chores, eat three square meals a day, play and sleep in a clean, comfortable bed. After so long sleeping on the floor it would take a long time for me to get used to this comfy bed.

Even though we girls were clearly happy with this reunion, it was obvious the split in our family had taken its toll on John. He seemed quiet, sad and withdrawn. We all missed Ron but I think the loss of him was particularly hard on John. After all he was our big brother and now he was gone. Whenever we asked about him we were told not to worry, he was fine.

Two

Our foster parents, whom we called Grandma and Grandpa, had a daughter Ada, who had recently been divorced and moved back home with her eight-year-old daughter, Bonnie. Then there was Emeretta, who was old, skinny, and mean, and was just there but added nothing to the household. I never really figured out if she was a friend or relative. When Grandma would go out and leave us with Emmeretta, she would always find ways in which we did something wrong. She would chase us with an iron frying pan and fortunately we could run faster! Later Ray, Ada's fiancé, would move in and share a room with John. When all was said and done there were nine of us in a four-bedroom house. My brother John lucked out because, as a boy, he had his own room until Ray came. Gerry, Pauline, and I shared a room. Emmeretta had the adjoining room, and Bonnie and Ada shared a makeshift space off the living room. Grandma and Grandpa were in the master bedroom.

Although it was a lot to digest, I felt we would be okay in this foster home, and as it turns out, we were. For the first time, it felt like some of the fractures in our little family were beginning to heal. It was as close to normal as I had felt in a long time or ever for that matter. I found myself looking over my shoulder less and less. Until this point I was a nervous little kid. I was always doubtful of things people told me, wary of their motives and most of all slept very little. Sleeping left me and my sister vulnerable and I learned to be on guard.

This was home such as it was. In time, each of us were able to develop a greater sense of self, even a feeling of security. We have our Grandma and Grandpa to thank for that. Also, we had routine, something that had been missing from our lives. There was school, chores and the Second Kent Baptist Church. As it was for most families in Holmes, New York church was a big part of our lives. It provided both a social life and a support system. If we hadn't chosen to be part of the world of church (not to imply we had a choice) we would not have had much of a life at all. With church friends we would go to the roller skating rink where I learned to skate. It was fun! We also would have ice skating parties on Stump pond across from our house, down by the parsonage. We would have roaring bond fires, cook hot dogs on a stick, roast marshmallows and drink hot coco. Life was shaping up for our little rag-tag family.

Yes, things were going well enough for all of us, but then I'd find myself thinking about my mother the woman I hadn't seen in a few years. When I would allow my thoughts to drift back to my mother I grew upset and uneasy. I thought about her a lot and was confused by her absence. I couldn't understand why she never came for us at the children's shelter after the fire. Could it be she really didn't love us? No that was impossible. Our mother loved us. Though, as time went by I began to think of her less and less. Yes, it would have been wonderful if she came and got us and took us home. We could have been a real family again and maybe things would be better and maybe Herman would be gone and maybe she would learn to be a real mom. Aah, but that never happened and now I am so grateful she didn't come and get us a thought that still makes me sad. As time passed our life was turning out to be much better than expected. Not perfect but better. We not only survived but we were thriving. I was still that tall skinny kid with the funny teeth and thick glasses but I was starting to think I mattered. However, it would take much longer for me to let my guard down.

So this was our life: church on Sunday morning and Sunday evening. Wednesday night Bible class and Friday night Young People's Meeting. That left Monday, Tuesday, and Thursday for homework and chores. Chores consisted of laundry on Monday before school, done in a washer with a hand wringer, which would wring out most of the water. We then hung the clothes out on the line even in the winter when the clothes froze so hard you thought they would break when you took them off the line. When we fussed about having to hang the clothes out in the freezing weather, Grandma just smiled.

"Now, now don't you fuss about freezing the clothes" she said.

"It makes ironing them easier." Well I was glad to hear that, since ironing was my job. Grandma's daughter, Ada, worked and told me she would give me 25 cents a basket to iron her clothes. I jumped at the chance, until I learned she wanted everything starched as well. However, I took the job (my first paying one) which meant I always had candy money for me and my siblings.

In the spring, fall and summer we would put out big buckets to catch rainwater. I thought it was a silly practice. Well in the summer the well would go dry and we had to use water sparingly and wash our hair with rainwater. We didn't like that and when we complained, Grandma would tell us,

"Hush, rainwater is God's hair conditioner." Also the shortage of water meant that we had to use the outhouse, and believe me, there was nothing Grandma could say to convince me that that was a good thing! We were one of the lucky families; we had a two-seater, one for kids and one for adults. There were two vent openings near the ceiling and it was very dark in there. Let me just say you would not bring a newspaper in with you. When you were in there it was just you and odors of others! My brother John had the job of shoveling out the outhouse when it got too full. Poor John! Gerry and I always had the job of setting the table and cleaning up after meals. I did the ironing, and in the summer, if something was particularly hard to iron, I would put it in the freezer for awhile. It did make it easier to iron! In the summer we weeded the garden, picked vegetables, and cleaned them for meals. We would also fish in stump pond for dinner. We would catch sunfish, scale them, cut off the head, gut them and fry them up for dinner. They were very tasty. On the weekend we cleaned the house and gathered everyone's dirty laundry to be ready for Monday. It sounds like drudgery even as I describe it but compared to what life had been like before; this was actually not so bad.

I remember the first day my sister and I attended our new school and how scared we were. I think now, years later, of when my son first went to school. I went with him to make sure that the experience would be a good one. Before the term began we visited the school and I showed him everything he would need to know about it. Where the office was. The cafeteria. I even took him into the boy's room so he would know about multiple toilets. I took him to the nurse's office and the main office, we had a wonderful tour and when his first day of school came he was a pro. When he got home from school he told me he helped a kid who was scared that day. I was delighted. It was not like that for Gerry and me. Grandma just hollered upstairs.

"The bus is here hurry up."

As we got off the bus at our new school, there was no one to meet us so we just wandered into the building not knowing where to go. As we were wandering around the halls, an adult spotted us and took us to the office. We sat there for a long time before anyone called us in. When we were called into the counselor's office, the guidance counselor wasn't quite sure what to do with us. There were no school records transferred, since we never attended formal school, just the school at the shelter. They had to determine how much we knew or did not know and what grade to place us in. The school psychologist did multiple tests and it was decided that Gerry would be placed in second grade and I would be in fourth. It was a struggle since I could barely read and Gerry didn't read at all. There were only four months left before the school year ended so they gave Gerry special reading help and decided to keep me in fourth grade the following year. There was just too much for me to learn in four months. It all felt so impersonal. There were conversations back and forth about us but never with us.

"Well I think this one should be placed in the second grade with some reading help," someone said, indicating Gerry.

"And the older one put her if forth for now and we'll see," someone else said. No one ever asked how we were doing or did we understand anything. They treated us as people had been doing our entire life as if we were invisible. As I was escorted to my classroom I felt so overwhelmed, I just wanted the day to be over. The halls were very crowded with kids who never looked my way. *Invisible*. When I finally arrived at the classroom the counselor opened the door and it was filled with kids.

When he opened the door he announced to the class.

"We have a new student."

That would be me. Not one person looked in my direction. *Invisible*. Everyone seemed not to hear him and continued doing what they were doing. I took a seat but no one talked to me. Everyone had their friends and groups and no one invited me in. When lunchtime came I sat alone at a big table, thinking someone would sit next to me; no one did. Gerry was not at the same lunch period but she told me later that she had made a friend. I was happy for her but a little jealous too. We somehow got through the day, but it was clear we would be on our own. In fact, throughout our entire school experience we had one reminder after another that we were not like everyone else. We were foster kids. Grandma always signed notes to the school as *Hazel T. Ketchum, Foster Mother.* Since everyone knew who she was, I wonder why she had to do that. It just drove home the point over and over that we were *those foster kids.*

I don't mean to imply that every day was a difficult one. There were fun ones, too. A particularly funny day was in December 1952. I was coming down the stairs and all of a sudden I stopped dead in my tracks. Grandma was dragging a pine tree into the house. I went running back upstairs to get Gerry, John and Pauline and told them I thought the old lady had lost her mind. We crept back down the stairs and sat in amazement. What was she doing? The four of us, holding on to the stair railing, our eyes so big and our mouths hanging open. We would learn later that what grandma was dragging in the house was called a Christmas tree.

"What is a Christmas tree?" I asked.

"Oh stop being so silly, you know what a Christmas tree is." She stood leaning on the banister, tired from her trek to and from the yard.

"No I don't," I said.

Grandma just looked at me.

"You are serious, aren't you?" She had no idea that we did not know about Christmas. We had our first Christmas celebration on December 25, 1952, and we even got presents. On Christmas morning John, Gerry, Pauline and I got up at the crack of dawn and ran down to the living room. The tree was lit and there seemed to be hundreds of packages wrapped in colorful paper under it. As the four of us stood there looking at the tree we had a group hug. We were startled by voices crying "ho, ho, ho."

In came Grandma, Grandpa, Ada, Bonnie and Emeretta. Before you knew it there was paper flying all over the place, boxes being opened and lots of screams of joy. We got clothes, toys and most of all I loved the red mirror, brush and comb for my dresser. It was great! I am sure this is why Christmas remains my favorite holiday. All the kids, grandkids and many friends join us at our home on Christmas Eve. I love it and never does a Christmas pass that I don't think about Grandma dragging in that pine tree and how amazed we kids were at the sight of it.

As we plowed through the years, many days were not easy for any of us. We felt different from the other kids and were not accepted by most of the kids. It would be a long time before I made any real friends. If I sat by someone in the lunch room, they got up and moved. If I dared to speak to someone, they either told me to shut up or walked away. When I was in the fifth grade, there was a birthday party and I was the only kid in the class who was not invited. In the girls' locker room I overheard someone say that it was because I was the foster kid. I sat in that bathroom stall until everyone had gone. I was so ashamed to come out and face my classmates.

"Those foster kids never have any money for a birthday present," the birthday girl said to the others. She was right, because if I had been invited, my foster mother would have told me that I could not attend because there was no money for a gift.

Some days were vague and seem to run together in my memory. But other days I recall quite clearly. Like the afternoon when we got off the bus and raced each other up the walk to the porch as we always did. The kitchen was curiously quiet Pauline had always been there to meet us and was anxious to play; but that day she was not there.

"Where's Pauline?" I asked, looking up the stairs. Perhaps she was ill.

"You kids better sit down," Grandma said. She pulled out a chair and sat down. My stomach flipped.

"I am afraid Pauline is gone for good."

"What!" Gerry screamed.

"What do you mean, gone for good?" I could hardly breathe. My heart was hammering in my chest. Gerry looked to me for answers.

Grandma spoke very softly and told us our mother had come with Herman and they took her away. I could not believe what I had just heard. Gerry was stomping around the kitchen out of control. *This can't be true, oh God tell us this is not true.* I cry even today as I write this I will never get over that moment; nor do I think will Gerry.

"Pauline was crying when she left," Grandma said, her eyes tearing.

"She wanted to wait for the bus."

"Oh my God why, why would they take her, they don't even like kids." I slammed my hand on the table.

"Grandma, can we get her back?" I was furious, holding my head in my hands, and then walking back and forth from the door to the kitchen sink.

"No Joanne, I am afraid we can't. They had papers and everything they needed to take her."

Then it dawned on me.

"Well, mom is our parent too. So why didn't she to take us?"

"I don't know, Joanne, but she didn't." Grandma's voice trailed off and eventually Gerry stopped crying. We sat there in silence I was thinking maybe it was a mistake. But I knew better. Mom loved men more than she loved us. Pauline was Herman's child and we were not. I finally accepted it. My mother didn't love me nor did anyone else. I had no value. I was worthless. As a mother today, this pain remains so vivid. Would I ever get over this feeling of rejection, of loss?

That evening as Gerry and I sat the dinner table we included Pauline's place setting a ritual we repeated for several nights. We would talk about her and wonder where she was and if she was eating dinner at the same time we were. The stories would eventually bring one or all of us to tears.

"Joanne you need to stop putting Pauline's place setting on the table." Grandma finally said.

"She is gone and we all have to get used to it."

"I know Grandma, but I miss her so much and I pretend she is sitting there." I knew she was right so I stopped. I did, however, take her fork and spoon to put them in a safe place with my stuff. We ultimately took her chair away from the table because we would just stare at it and begin to cry. One day while cleaning our room, I found a pair of her little corduroy pants in the drawer upstairs and slept with them under my pillow for many, many months. I would fall asleep with thoughts of her in my head. I felt that if I could keep something of hers close to me then I could protect her. I could not. Pauline was just three years old at the time. She was so cute; we called her Whistle Britches because of the way her corduroy pants "whistled" when her legs brushed together as she walked. We had grown close to her and now she was yanked away for good. We believe we would never see her again. Pauline would suffer a life of confusion and pain which I would not know about for 40 years.

It was a heartbreaking moment when we were told that Pauline's father had taken her. He and our mother were going to live in Alabama. We learned later that when they got there, Pauline was placed in an orphanage. As she grew up, she was told she was the only child of a woman who had died giving birth to her. This would have its long-term effects on her. It is my belief that Herman was so angry with mom for placing Jamie up for adoption without telling him, that he would get back at her through Pauline. Jamie had been born several months after Pauline was placed in our foster home. So in an effort to get back at mom he tricked her into thinking they would live a happy life in Alabama. I knew Herman was an evil person but I did not believe he was capable of stooping this low. But he was! Mom stayed with him for a few years before she worked her way back to New York City. She got a sales job in a major department store and set up an apartment for herself. She never came to get us! That was our mother. She came first in her life and her children paid the price. She was a survivor and I guess that is one good quality she passed on to us. I'm glad I learned that from her. As it turns out, I've had to face more than my share of difficult times and that survival quality has been very helpful.

Years later I would learn that mental health professionals would classify my mother, as a narcissistic personality, someone totally self-centered and an expert manipulator. My mother was from Tampa Florida and had little education. She was, as they say, not the sharpest tack in the box. She was, however, a survivor: the daughter of Jamie Brown and Tim Jackson, the only girl with two older brothers, Tim and Bobby. Her mother, my grandmother, died very young as a result of tuberculosis and my grandfather moved back to the Grand Cayman Island after her death. My mother does not remember her mother she was just a baby when she died. She also did not know that she had two older brothers. After her own mother's death, my mother was placed in a foster home. Mr. and Mrs. Dolphin, friends of the family took her in. Her brothers Tim and Bob were placed with family members. Mom never understood why her family did not take her in as they did her brothers. She never really got over being abandoned and in the end she did the same to us.

To say our mother had a difficult life was a bit of an understatement. She was raised by two people who treated her as if she was their personal housekeeper. Ultimately, she was repeatedly sexually abused by her foster father. That fact troubled me many years later when she insisted on purchasing a headstone for his grave.

When she was about 15, she was eventually told she had two brothers. Later she located them and got to know them and their families. She never talked much about them to us as a matter of fact; she never told us she had siblings until after they had died.

I wonder if people ever take into consideration the fallout when they break up a family. Do they ever consider consulting the children as to how we will feel? Of course not. Do they ever think how their decisions will play out in our lives? Of course they do not. The decisions that were made for my mother and the decisions my mother ultimately made for her children will impact our lives. Our wants and needs, as always, counted for very little. The day Pauline was snatched from us was a horrific day. I remember crying so much that my eyes were almost swollen shut. I looked so bizarre that the next day I had to stay home from school. After that loss, I started to look over my shoulder again. How long would it be before someone came to take another one of us away? This was hard on the whole household. Pauline had been pure joy and now the joy was gone. We had been pawns in a chess game. In our world, people could take you, move you around or do whatever they felt like with you. Any feelings of security had been ripped from my soul. It would take me decades to trust to feel secure again. This was a defining moment in my life, one of overwhelming pain and sorrow. Somewhere in my young and impressionable consciousness, this event, like many others, would create a deep furrow that would later cause me trauma, cause me to make bad decision, and would ultimately damage my health. I realize now we pay a price for everything we go through. The price we pay is high or low, depending upon how we process the ups and downs of life.

As our daily routine slowly returned to something that resembled normal, we struggled to understand what happened to Pauline and to us. But somehow understanding never came, at least not during my youth. Only now, as I look back on events can I make sense out of some of them. Some still make no sense. John, for example, was treated much more harshly than we were when we broke the rules. When he was a teenager and should have been eating he wasn't. Where we were raised there was breakfast, lunch, and dinner and nothing in between. We did not know the word "snack." Being a growing boy and hungry all the time, John went next door to his friend's house and helped himself to some fruit pies. He later confessed to this deed when the neighbor came over and told our foster mother that the pies were missing. As a result John got a beating like we had never seen. Grandma called all of us into the kitchen and told us what John had done. As we watched in horror she beat him with her hands. She was a big woman and very strong from working around the property and in the garden. We had never experienced this violent side of Grandma before. We had had spankings before for breaking the rules but nothing like this. Hit after hit he eventually dropped to the floor and crawled under the kitchen sink to try to escape her repeated blows. As this assault continued John never made a sound. It was as if he refused to let her know that she was hurting him. I think that made her even angrier and the hits got harder and faster. Then Grandpa joined in on the assault and he was carrying a razor strap. Now, John was screaming, Gerry, Bonnie (Ada's daughter) and I clung to each other shaking uncontrollable. I felt as if I were going to throw up. We all stood there with tears running down our faces not making a peep. We had never seen such a demonstration of pure fury.

"Stop" I cried.

"You're killing him."

Grandma turned her red face to us.

"Be quiet or you'll be next." She turned back to John.

"Stealing is not acceptable," she roared. Our foster parents seemed to think if you beat a child with a razor strap, it would be a more meaningful punishment, and the child would not forget why he had gotten the beating. Well she was right about that because that beating remains burned in my memory and I am sure in my brother's. These were different times. If this were happening today, we kids would have been immediately removed from the home and our foster mother and father would have been arrested. These incidents still bring on tears when I think of them.

The fallout from that day had a huge effect on all of us. Gerry and I were much more obedient knowing now how angry Grandma could get. John, however, never got over the humiliation of that beating. It was at this time that he began to rebel and took on the attitude of not caring and who could blame him? He would climb out of his window to meet his friends. When Grandma found out she nailed the window shut so he could not get back in. When he would return he would sleep on the porch. I think even Grandma knew this was the beginning of the end for the two of them. John was almost 17. A few months later he did what a lot of young men in this situation do he ran off and joined the navy. My sister and I did not know this until it happened. John had been rebelling and staying away from home so we only saw him in school and that's when he decided to attend class. Again, it was one of those arrivals from school when we were told of his leaving.

As we walked through the kitchen door dragging our book bags behind us and carrying the mail Grandma made her announcement.

"Well, I guess we won't have to worry about Johnny anymore; he's in the Navy." I could not believe what I was hearing.

"What the heck is going on?" I ran to see if his stuff was gone from his room. It was still there, she must be kidding. I ran back down stairs and into the kitchen. As we stood there I asked why and was told that my guess was as good as hers. She said she did not know but we did not believe her. The Navy would not take a 17 year old without telling someone. Or did they?

"You're kidding, right?" I said.

"No Joanne, your brother joined the Navy last week and shipped out today." I was stunned. He never mentioned a word. I guess he was afraid I would tell someone. John was 17 and in the 1950's you did not need your parents' signature to join the service.

"He's in the United States Navy now!" I considered it. We stood there with our mouths open and just starred at her. She then announced it was time to do our chores.

"Oh, by the way, there will be no further discussion about this subject." She fanned herself with a magazine. A few weeks later we got a letter from John and we were on cloud nine, just knowing that he was okay. It served him well. He went on to have a successful Navy career and learned many life skills as a result of his enlistment.

Grandpa died in February, 1958. He had always been a quiet man, a carpenter by trade. He went to work every day and came home every night. He would eat supper, then go out into the garage and putter for a bit, drink some Bromo-Seltzer, and go to bed. He suffered from a temperamental stomach. He was a kind man who had no say in anything that went on at home, and didn't have much say in our lives. But I remember, he would always pat me on the head and say,

"Remember, it's very important that you finish school." And that was it. No further discussion about school or anything else for that matter. I always got the feeling that he cared but was unable to show it. It was only during John's beating that any of us ever saw his violent side. I never wanted to find out what might make him become that violent person again.

Grandpa came down with an illness that afflicted his kidneys which in turn forced him to be hospitalized for a very long time. We would visit him with Grandma. Usually Ada, drove us because Grandma didn't drive. Every time we went to see him he seemed stronger and stronger. When Grandma left the hospital March 9, 1958 they told her she could bring him home the next day. Then that night the call came. She listened, hung up the phone and stared. The silence was deafening.

"He's gone," Grandma said and began to weep. She was stunned and saddened and as she wept, we wept with her.

Grandpa's death would change our lives. No one was expecting it, especially Grandma! The funeral was a few days later, March 12, 1958. I was amazed at all the people who came to the house. They brought food and just kept talking, trying to distract Grandma from the pain and fear of what the future would hold for all of us. With the coming and going of all those guests, I realized many people had loved this unassuming, *quiet man.*

Grandpa's passing was more important than it actually seemed at the time and would have a direct impact upon us. With Grandpa gone, Grandma was not sure that the Leake & Watts Children Home would allow her, a widow, to keep two teenage girls. Ironically, we had just been starting to feel comfortable and secure with our placement and feeling that we finally belonged somewhere. Would it be time to go to another foster home?

The prospect of being uprooted again left us feeling unsettled for several days. Then, on a bitter cold day in March, with snow falling and the wind blowing with a vengeance, a social worker paid us a visit. As our school bus approached the house I noticed a strange car parked in the driveway. I grabbed Gerry's hand and pointed it out. As we walked up the walk to the house we were chatty and appeared happy. I thought this demeanor would be best. We burst through the kitchen door and tossed our book bags on the floor.

"Hey Grandma, we're home," I said. The social worker was sitting at the kitchen table with Grandma. They looked serious.

Grandma instructed us to sit at the table. She told us the social worker needed to speak to us privately. Grandma left the room and the social worker got right to the point.

"Okay girls, here's the question. Do you want to continue to live here with Grandma or would you like the agency to place you elsewhere? I will give you girls some privacy to talk. Call me when you are ready." She left the room and Gerry and I just stared at each other. We were in shock that we were being given a choice. For the first time in our lives, someone was asking us what we wanted. We couldn't believe it!

"Well Gerry, how do you feel about making a life changing decision today?" Gerry started to laugh and put her finger to her brow tapped a couple of times and then moved her finger to her cheek.

"Well let me see, what shall we do?" We stayed in there far longer than we needed to but were relishing the moment. After some discussion and weighing of choices, Gerry and I decided it would be better to stay, simply because we did not know where we would be sent. We called her back to the kitchen and Gerry and I told her that we wanted to stay. She asked why.

"Well, we know life here and have gotten use to it. We have some friends in school and are comfortable there. Starting over in a new home and new school would be real hard." It was a rare privilege to be given a choice and it was amazing to us that we had had a chance to express our opinion to someone who was listening.

With Grandma we knew what the components of our lives were and what we could expect day to day. If we elected to leave, we might be made to live with our mother. That option had not been brought up and I wanted to make sure it would not come up. No, no, no… that thought was way too scary.

It's a good thing we remained with Grandma, because although we did not realize it, at the time, the tables were turning. For a change, she needed us and the monthly check we brought in. She received $80 per month for each of us and back in the 50s that was big money. So our staying served everyone involved.

At this point of my life, other things were also changing. Ada married Ray and she and her daughter Bonnie moved into the home Grandpa built for them next door. As I mentioned John had already left and joined the Navy. There were fewer people in the house now and money was tight. Like all teenagers, I wanted more for myself and also wanted to help out our family financially so I took the first step. I decided to make getting a job a win-win situation.

I was already enrolled in the business program at the high school and if I got a job in the business field, I would be evaluated each semester and receive course credits for experience. That is exactly what I did. I got a job in a local land surveyor's office as a secretarial assistant and not only took home a paycheck, but received course credits at the same time. I went to school until noon and worked from 12:30 to 5 pm every day. For the first time in my life I felt like a contributing member of society, able to pay for my keep. I did feel very grown-up; I even got to wear high heels to work!

In truth, I was the office gofer. Sometimes the guys in the office would play tricks on me. I remember one day one of the guys was complaining that he could not find his lunch. Another suggested I had filed it away.

"Hey, you know Joanne files everything so efficiently" he said. If anyone needed anything, it was my job to get it. I filed all the correspondence and client files, typed letters and after a while I was even allowed to write the letters and sign the bosses' name. Wow I had arrived! Sometimes I think about those days and realize it was the beginning of the growth of my self-esteem, however, that growth would take a very long time.

When I turned 16, I was determined to learn to drive. But in order to apply for a learner's permit I would need my birth certificate. Through our years in foster care we had had occasional visits from mom and kept in touch with her through letters. At this stage of my life I was still very angry at her but I wrote and asked her to send me a copy of the document. Patiently, I waited and waited, checking the mail every day. It seemed like I was waiting an eternity but it was probably only a few months when I realized the birth certificate would never arrive. I was angry and frustrated. But then Grandma told us that our mother was coming to visit and she would bring my birth certificate with her.

Once again, I had figured out how to get what I wanted. It was just another sunny day and I went to school as usual. As the school day progressed, I felt uneasy about seeing my mom. It would have been much easier if she just sent my birth certificate as I'd asked. I really was confused why she would come up in the middle of the week, in the past she'd always visited on a Sunday. After work I caught my ride home with my neighbor. Gerry stayed after school and rode home with us. My neighbor dropped us off and we went into the house. I sensed right away something was different. I don't know why I felt so unsettled because everything looked normal when we entered the house. Maybe I felt unsettled because I really didn't want to see my mother.

Grandma was sitting in her rocker in the kitchen as we opened the door. She summoned us into the living room.

"I have someone for you to meet." As we entered the living room, we saw mom standing there with a man. I did not think anything of him. He was not the first man we had seen her with, nor would he be the last. Mom seemed nervous. We all just looked at each other.

"Joanne, I would like you to meet your father," my mother said. *My father? He died in the war, I thought. Suddenly he was there risen from the dead, standing in Grandma's living room, how could that be?* He was a large man with grey hair that was going white. He looked to be more than six feet tall and was round around the middle. I was acutely aware that I looked a lot like him. He seemed as nervous as Mom maybe even more, but then he smiled and extended his hand. I did not return the gesture.

Wow, my father. I should have been excited, but I wasn't. I was afraid he might take me away, as Pauline's father had done.

"Hi, nice to meet you," I replied, and then left the room. I went upstairs, Gerry tagging along after me. The grownups just stood silently as we left the room.

"Is he my father too?" Gerry asked as we climbed the stairs to our room.

"I don't think so," I replied quietly.

"Does that mean we're not sisters?" I took her by the shoulders.

"Oh my God, absolutely not; we will always be sisters." I felt so bad for Gerry who looked sad and scared, as if she knew something bad was going to happen the way it always had. Everyone in the room had acted as though she were invisible; no one said hello to her. Being a quiet child, she said nothing herself. We sat on our beds trying to hear the conversation downstairs but we heard only muffled voices. I was so proud of myself for turning and leaving, but also fearful I would be punished for that act of defiance. I didn't care. I couldn't believe my mother would have staged this meeting and not taking anyone's feelings into account. But what about Gerry's feelings? I had to remind myself, it was always all about mom. This was her grandstanding once again and getting it all wrong. We were not quite sure what to do. Should we go downstairs or stay in our room? We decided to stay in our room. Gerry was asking why he was not her father. I could not answer that. About a half an hour passed and Grandma called us downstairs.

"You will both be going to dinner with your mother and Jack," she said.

"Why?" I demanded to know. Grandma cleared her throat.

"Your mother wants to spend some time with you girls."

"Do we have to go?" Gerry asked.

"Yes, go wash your hands, comb your hair and be quick about it." As we left it was a quiet ride to the restaurant. I had never been to a restaurant and going with my mother for the first time to one was not exactly what I had in mind. I was so angry and determined not to be much fun. I was still fuming over the scene in the living room. So off we went. My mother was very chatty but we said nothing. We arrived at the restaurant and piled out of the car. The restaurant was beautifully decorated and very elegant. It was not a place where we felt comfortable. It was early and we were the only patrons and there we sat not having a clue what to say or do. The waitress brought us menus and Gerry and I looked at them and had no idea what to order. It was a French restaurant and we could not read the menu. Mom asked us what we wanted and we told her something with chicken. She ordered us something we couldn't pronounce. For herself she ordered a strange sounding dish with something on the side. My new found father would have the same. How sweet! As we sat there my mind wandered back to the living room scene and I got angry that mom thought so little of our feelings. Well how would she, I reasoned. She didn't even know us. I felt awkward and thought Jack felt that way too, but Mom seemed to be quite delighted. I watched my father as mom took charge of the dinner conversation; he went from awkward to uncomfortable and out of place. This man was my father and I could care less. For years, I wondered what he would look like, if he were short or tall and now, in this moment none of that mattered. I watched her in action; it was as if she were auditioning for a part in life. The part of our mother. As we sat there, I thought, oh please, please, please don't let me grow up to be like her. I think she imagined herself taking Gerry and me away and we would all live happily ever after. She must have fantasized that once Jack, who we would find out later, was still *married* at the time, once he met me, his daughter, he would divorce his wife and marry her. That did, in fact, happen but not for another 16 years. I couldn't wait for this evening to be over so I could get back home.

The next day it was confirmed that Jack was my father but not Gerry's.

"What about everyone else?" I asked, only wanting to know just how many fathers we all had. Grandma had implied Ron, John and Gerry all had the same father. I felt like an outcast, the only oddball. But we would find out much later that what Grandma had thought was also not true.

When we got back from our night out, my mother finally gave me the important birth certificate, my reward for being civil to her, I guess. It was then that I saw that my name was different from what I had thought it was. For 16 years I had been Joanne Jackson but overnight I became Joanne Keane.

"Joanne Keane?" I asked.

"Who's that?"

"That's you," My mother was straight-faced, as if I were asking a ridiculous question.

Could life possibly get more complicated?!

"Well girls, we must get back to the city, it's a long ride." My father walked over to me, gave me a peck on the cheek and turned to leave. It was amazing they gave kisses and hugs and headed out the door. Not a word from my father about where he has been all my life or what his intentions are now. I think I knew, and I was right, he had none.

"Oh, it was nice meeting you," he said. Nice meeting me I thought, you have got to be kidding, I'm your daughter, not just anybody. I should have known that something was about to happen. After all, mom rarely visited us. She tried to get up to see us on holidays and even then she didn't always make it.

The following week I went to the motor vehicle bureau and applied for my learner's permit. I did get it and it would be the first of many times I would have to remember my new name.

That would be the easy part. On Monday I had to go to the high school office and start the process of changing my last name from Jackson to Keane. Oh, the questions I was asked! Like a lot of foster children, I had been trying to keep a low profile, and now I had to explain why my sister and I had different last names. Once again, my mother had managed to make my life difficult and this would hardly be the last time. Wasn't it bad enough that as a foster kid I had been made to feel less than worthy? Now I had to deal with this.

For the first 16 years of my life I had lived as Joanne Jackson and now I found that she had not really existed. I had been living a lie, unwittingly operating under an assumed name. I wasn't who I said I was or who I was told I was. Then I started to wonder how Gerry and the rest of my siblings would feel about me once they learned I was not their full blood sister. Little did I know that none of us were full blood siblings, except for Pauline and Jamie, who were born to the same set of parents.

During the next couple of months, mom became more interested in seeing her daughters. She visited more often and we were suspicious rightfully so. We soon learned that Mom wanted us to leave Grandma and move to New York with her. I guess she was getting ready to begin her plan to reel my biological father into her life but first she had to set the stage. Gerry and I would be the main props she would use in her plan. One day she paid us a surprise visit. We arrived home from school and found her with Grandma at the kitchen table.

"I'm ready to take my girls home," we heard our mother say.

I felt like I was going to be sick. Thank God John had joined the Navy and was no longer subject to her wishes and whims. But I wasn't going to let her get away with this. Gerry and I had a quick conference and concluded that we did not like this plan. Now the question remained how to tell her.

As we sat down for dinner that night, the dreaded topic came up.

"So girls, what would you think about moving to New York and living with me?"

Mom passed the peas and smiled. We looked at her. She cleared her throat.

"You know I have worked very hard to get back on my feet so I could bring you girls home."

"We are home," I said, finally. We had been told our mother had tuberculosis and couldn't care for us. I had known this was a lie. Now she was telling us she worked hard to get on her feet. I wondered if she was 'on her feet' the day she snatched Pauline from our home.

"Well, Joanne." Mom straightened her shoulders.

"This was only a temporary home." Grandma flashed a look at mom but said nothing. She then looked at me.

"Isn't temporary a few days or months?" Grandma asked.

"We've been here for over seven years," I said.

"I am not sure but I think that's more than temporary." My mother sighed and dropped the subject. It seemed there was still room for negotiation and no decisions would be made that night. Gerry, as always, remained silent through dinner. I asked if we could have some time to think about it. A few days later, though, we wrote mom a letter, sparing her feelings by using the excuse that with Grandpa gone, Grandma needed us now more than ever. We also told her we wanted to graduate with our friends, even though that was a few years off. Surprisingly, mom accepted our decision and continued on her way. Our decision may have broken what was left of her heart but I doubt it. I always suspected that deep down mom did not want the responsibility of two teenage girls. And why would we have wanted to live with her? I hate to think what our life would have been like if we had been with her all those years. My feeling was that she was trying to set a trap for my father, hoping that if she concocted a family setting that included Gerry and I he would be encouraged to leave his wife. Oddly enough, when he finally did capitulate and freed himself to marry her, it was without Gerry and me in the picture at all.

No, Gerry and I preferred to stay where we were. The lives we had led played a role in determining the young adults we now were. I had come to appreciate the predictable life we had had at Grandma's. John's beating aside; she really did want what was best for us. She was not a loving, affectionate person, but she taught us to follow the rules so we could survive. She also made sure we went to school and graduated.

After that, life by our standards was uneventful on Ludingtonville Road. However there were always discussions that involved money or the lack of it. Since I had been lucky enough to land that job in the surveyor's office, I was able to contribute financially. When I graduated high school, college was not an option. I was hired full-time in the surveyor's office and my business career was on its way. It would have been great to go to college, and I had dreams of attending law school, but things did not unfold that way. Later in life I took the college courses I needed to be successful in my business career. However, in the very early 1960s, if you were in foster care and you finished high school, you were on your own.

So I fell into the trap that was a way of thinking in those years: you went out on your own or you got married. I married the first guy who asked me. The way it unfolded was characteristic of my history.

Three

Like many young women of my time, I married for all the wrong reasons. While still in high school, I became engaged to Norman, who later jilted me. Then I married another man on the rebound. But I'm getting ahead of myself.

Norman and I had met in church. Where else would we meet? He was my first love and I was very smitten. He was tall with jet black hair, also kind and patient and very family oriented, which was important to me. I saw myself as part of his family very early on and his siblings, parents and relatives eagerly gathered me into the fold. For the first time, I was accepted for who I was and that made me feel wonderful.

Ours was a comfortable relationship that went on for about two years. Norman was in the military and soon to be stationed over in Korea. Before he left, he gave me an engagement ring. It was a solitaire quarter carat diamond but in my eyes it was the most beautiful ring I had ever seen. It represented so much more to me than a piece of jewelry. He came home on leave now and again and we would spend time with his family, which created a feeling of security and cemented our future together. We spent hour after hour talking about where we wanted to live and how many kids we would have. For the first time, life seemed to be in my control. But I was to find out that it was all an illusion. I am afraid I got too comfortable and forgot for a time I was the person that no one really wanted. While Norman was in the service, we wrote to each other every day. But then I started to receive love letters written in Korean, with affectionate phrases. What was this? I was suspicious, wondering where Norman was learning these romantic bits and pieces of the language.

After Norman was gone for another eight months or so, his sister sat with me in church one Sunday. Just before the benediction, she turned and whispered in my ear.

"Oh Joanne, I don't know how to tell you this?" I blinked. What was she telling me? Was he hurt? What was she keeping from me?

"Norman is seeing a Korean girl." She patted me on the back and picked up her bible.

That was how he came to learn all those romantic phrases. I got up placed the hymnal back, walked down the aisle, down the church steps and started home. I was crying when a friend pulled up alongside and offered to drive me home. I accepted the ride but couldn't find the words to tell her what was wrong. When I got home I decided to write and ask if in fact this was true. His answer would confirm what his sister had told me. As I had dreaded and waited, no reply came. So I accepted that Norman was now involved with another woman. His mother came to the house to collect the ring and some of Norman's personal items and I was less than polite when I threw the ring across the room. Norman's mother was very upset.

"Have a great day!" I said on her way out the door. She was a lovely person and I knew she loved me. She felt as bad about this as I did.

Of course, I was devastated by this rejection. I thought this would be the end of me, that maybe I would find my heart lying on the pillow all broken and unfixable. As I lay on my bed crying my eyes out, I felt that this was what my life would be like. I was worthless and why would anyone want me anyway? I would have to get use to rejection after rejection, reminding myself time and again that I had no worth. How could I know what a great relationship was?

And so unfortunately, I married the next person who came along Everett who I also met in church. He had just broken up with his former girlfriend, who just happened to be Norman's sister. This was not an unusual occurrence in small town life, where people were closely connected though community channels. When Everett asked me to accompany him to the stock car races the following Saturday night, I accepted. Why not? I had just been jilted and was anxious to end that hurt. I thought that being with someone else would do it. It did not, but that was not apparent at the start of the relationship. Besides, getting married to Everett would be my way out of my house, to finally be a grown-up. I am not proud of that decision, but I forgive myself for having made it because I was so young. I truly had no idea what constituted a good relationship, what I was supposed to feel or how I was expected to behave. What I did know was that time after time I learned I had no value (not to mention self-esteem) and I better take the first one who comes along.

On my wedding day, I sat on my bed staring out the window. The wind was blowing and it was cold and dank, and after a while a gentle snow began to fall, the snowflakes dancing silently to the frozen ground. I sat there wondering what the hell I was doing. All I wanted to do was crawl back under the covers and escape the day. It was December 15, 1962. I had told Grandma a few days earlier that I did not know if this was the right thing to do.

"Oh don't be silly you are just having pre-wedding jitters," she told me. That was yesterday. Now it was happening. What could I do at this late date? Invitations had been mailed. Food had been prepared and relatives were coming from long distances. Everett had aunts, uncles and cousins that would be attending the wedding. I was afraid to inconvenience anyone, so I got out of bed and went down to the kitchen. Gerry was there putting some finishing touches on the trays of finger foods we had prepared for the reception.

"Good morning" she said cheerfully and I returned the greeting not so cheerfully.

"What's wrong?" She asked.

I slumped down in the chair by the window. The snow was coming down exceptionally heavy now. I considered what I would do if we couldn't get to church.

"I just think I should be much more excited than I am today."

"Oh cheer up, you're just nervous." Gerry went about working on the finger food trays I moped around doing what was expected of me and before I knew it my brother Ron arrived with his wife Jean and we were on our way to the church.

Everett and I were married in the Second Kent Baptist Church, right in our own community. Outside, the snow was blowing. Despite the sizable snowfall, my mother managed to show up. There she was, being escorted down the aisle by the usher, the last to be seated. After all, she was the mother of the bride. She was impeccably dressed and gazed around the church as if she were royalty. She was on the arm of yet another boyfriend, Joe, and although this provoked many a question in the minds of guests, no one, including me said anything.

I had known Joe since I was about 17, but did not distinguish him much from all the others. I would learn years later that Joe was a second story man, a thief! Gerry and I used to come in contact with him whenever we visited our mother, usually whenever a new Elvis movie came out. As teenagers, seeing an Elvis movie would make these trips more tolerable. Joe always left in the middle of the night and returned to the apartment early in the morning. We never asked where he was or what he was doing, but perhaps we should have. Before we would leave he would sometimes give each of us a piece of jewelry. I just figured this was a kind of bribe, a way for Joe to buy our support or at least our silence. It didn't work; though. I instinctively knew he was not a good person. And this was the man my mother brought to my wedding! I still marvel at her audacity.

My brother Ron gave me away and my sister Gerry was my maid of honor. We had a small reception in the church hall, where guests ate finger food that Gerry and I had prepared. The snow was still going strong and we hurried the reception so guests could get safely home. Everett and I were ushered to our car and people threw rice and off we went. "Well we did it, we tied the knot" I said. He seemed apprehensive and was complaining bitterly about the weather. He was vigorously brushing the snow off his clothes, never glancing my way. As I sat there, looking over at my new husband, I was already regretting having gone through with this wedding. I knew I had made a terrible mistake. Hearing my Grandma's words in my ear made me cringe.

"You make your bed, you sleep in it," she'd say when we'd made a mistake.

After our wedding we took a short trip to the tri-state rock. I think I was supposed to be excited it was a place where there was this big rock that touched three states, New York, New Jersey and Pennsylvania. How exciting! It was a rock, that's it a rock. I put on my happy face and tried to enjoy the view. Remember it was December, cold, baron trees, no color to speak of just grey covered with snow. Wow! As I look back at that trip, I realize how pathetic my reaction was. This trip was, in fact, a preview of my marriage. In those first days together as a married couple, the writing was on the wall. I soon learned that it was his way or no way. I suggested a certain restaurant for dinner he had something else in mind. It was that way from that day forward. He would often tell me,

"Just remember I am always right and the only time I was wrong was when I was right and thought I was wrong." I think that sums it up. He made every decision and if I tried to contribute to any decision I was ignored. Two or three days later we returned to town and moved in with Grandma. We had no place to live and thought the extra rent would help her out. Surprisingly, she thought of this arrangement as taking in another foster kid, charging us $160 a month! Again, it was not like I was like everyone else. I was a product that brought in money and now I added to the cache by marrying Everett and bringing in another boarder. Wow, the things we do to avoid rejection. That was quite a steep rent in 1962 and so this situation could not last. We soon found a furnished studio apartment for $16 a week. We moved to our new home to begin our life as a married couple on our own. I had hoped that we would somehow connect as a couple and start out on a wonderful journey. I was wrong, however, determined to make it work.

Within three months I was expecting a baby. I was happy and excited, but my husband did not share my enthusiasm. Everett's cousin took me to the doctor where it was confirmed I was pregnant. As we drove back to her apartment I was so excited and began planning a wonderful dinner menu. Everett soon arrived at his cousin's apartment and I told him he was going to be a dad. He looked at me with disdain. He never said a word, just got in his car and drove off. His reaction came as a shock for I just assumed he had wanted a family as I did. He disappeared for two days and I wondered if he would actually return. There was no choice for me but to make the best of it, keep going, and hope he would have a change of heart. But he never did.

As the pregnancy progressed, I realized Everett wanted no part of this baby or for that matter, no part of the life we were supposedly building together. He had begun down a path of destructive behavior. One consolation was that my in-laws were delighted they were going to have a grandchild and time would show they would turn out to be the most wonderful and caring grandparents a child could hope for. From the beginning my son shared a closeness with them that was heartwarming. I could only hope that when the time came for me I would have the same kind of relationship with my grandchildren. I never really understood why Everett did not take to parenting. I believe it was his fear of taking responsibility that kept him from enjoying his role as a dad.

The following December I gave birth to a son with the biggest brown eyes I ever saw. We named him Everett, III. As I looked into those beautiful eyes, somehow I knew I had just received my greatest gift. I felt deeply that it would be just my baby and me for the long haul and when I left the hospital on Christmas day, it was the start of another adventure.

Motherhood came naturally to me and I loved it. I was determined to be the best mother ever and one thing was certain my son would never feel unloved. When Everett was only three weeks old, it was clear that he was not doing well. Every time I fed him he would projectile vomit and it was not long before he became quite weak from dehydration and malnourishment. I took him to every doctor in the area and described the problem. This was the start of a phenomenon that would haunt me into my later adult life; doctors who don't know what to do often do the wrong thing. Over and over again I was told that the problem was me.

"You are an anxious mother," they all said.

"You are making your baby sick." I knew this was not true and I was furious. With my experience as the eldest sister in a large family, I was very comfortable around babies and certainly not nervous with them.

Finally one Sunday after church, a woman who knew what I was going through suggested the name of her pediatrician, Dr. Martin Randolph, in Danbury, Connecticut. On Monday morning I called and made an appointment for that very afternoon. As I undressed Everett for the examination, and fed him a bottle as the doctor instructed, he showed me a roll across the baby's stomach. He explained that the tube that is supposed to direct the food into his stomach had slowly closed after birth. It was a rare condition, but the doctor must have seen this condition before because he recognized it immediately. He corroborated his suspicions by saying that it is usually found in first-born males. Dr.

Randolph very calmly told me that he would be operating within the hour.

"The prognosis is not good," he told me.

"When an infant is this small and this weak it causes other problems."

I was frantic but I tried to stay calm.

"What kind of problems?" I asked, afraid of the answer.

"It is very possible that there has already been irreversible brain damage." I stood not really hearing what was being said, except I knew it was bad. The room was a blur and spinning; I was going to throw up. Dr. Randolph continued to examine my son. He explained that

"When an infant undergoes anesthesia there is always risk however, with an infant less than five pounds and dehydrated, the risks are even greater." He was honest and said that he could not guarantee the results. He instructed me to bring the baby to the hospital immediately.

I was stunned, scared and angry. Finally, I had something in my life that was *good*, that was *mine*, and now I faced the chance of losing him. I dressed Everett and drove him to the hospital, only to be stopped by a traffic officer for going the wrong way on a one way street. Obviously my mind was numb. When I explained my situation to the officer, he pulled his car in front of mine.

"Follow me," he said. With sirens blaring, lights flashing, we rolled into the hospital.

I took that precious bundle to the admitting office. For most of this ordeal I was alone, but I did call my husband who finally arrived minutes before Everett was taken to surgery. As they wheeled him down the hall to the operating room, my heart turned to stone. I was convinced if he didn't make it I would never feel my heart again. Hours went by, and with each tick of the clock my hopes seemed to increase. I believed the longer it took, the better his chances were. This kind of thinking helped me to survive. When I tried to have a conversation with Everett about our son, he refused to talk about him.

"You know what the doc said," my husband, said,

"He probably won't survive so why talk about it?" I was devastated that he had given up on our son so quickly. However, deep down inside I knew that parenting was difficult for him. Hours later, when they wheeled my beautiful baby into the post-op room, my heart began to beat once again. The room was very large, filled with all kinds of equipment. The walls were decorated with nursery rhyme characters and the crib they put him in looked like a cage. I stood there looking down at him. He was pale, so tiny and breathing very rapidly. He never moved, not even his head. He only had on a diaper and there were tubes coming out of his nose, his stomach and his arms. The only thing that gave me hope was I could see his chest move up and down when he breathed. As soon as the nurses left the room, I slipped my hand into the crib to touch him; his skin soft and thin. I fantasized about holding him I knew if I could do that he would be okay.

I spent the next week by Everett's bed, waiting for the moment he would be able to keep food down. Until he could do that, the doctors would not let me take him home. It was hard to keep my spirits up with the kind of talk I was hearing from my husband and in-laws. They were convinced the baby would be brain damaged from malnourishment and dehydration and would need to be placed in a facility that would care for him.

In the hospital, day after day, as I sat by Everett's bed I became more and more hopeful. I would see a little curl in his lip or a glint in his eyes; I could not take my eyes off him. One afternoon as I sat watching that beautiful bundle, my husband said he needed to talk to me.

"Go ahead, I'm listening." At this point I really could care less about what he had to say. I was angry that he had given up on our son and would even entertain the thought that he might die.

"I know you don't want to hear this, but my folks and I have been talking and we think he should be put in a facility where he can get the best care."

"Have you lost your mind?" I glared at him.

"There is nothing wrong with this baby and I will be taking him home to care for him when the time comes." I knew that his only concern was being saddled with a child that would need special attention and lots of our time and he really did not want that. He was not concerned about me or our baby only himself as usual. I told both my husband and my in-laws, with great passion that if they did not want to be part of this endeavor, which I considered to be one of life's greatest privileges, they did not have to. I released them from all responsibility and vowed to take care for my son, if necessary, by myself.

"No one, I tell you, no one will ever take my son away from me. That is a promise." They just stood there and finally Everett's mother spoke.

"Joanne you must let go, it is God's will."

"Oh really, you think it is God's will? Well let me tell you, God and me don't see eye to eye on this one."

As they all turned and left, my mother-in-law came back in and told me she would help in any way she could.

Once Everett's intestinal problem was fixed, he grew and thrived and was, in fact, never really sick again. He was a bright chatty kid. He walked at ten months old and was speaking in two and three word sentences by the time he was a year. He loved life and his grandparents. We lived next door to my in-laws and when Everett was old enough he would check on dinner menus in each home to decide where he would rather have dinner. When I went back to work, my foster mother was delighted to babysit. Her name was Hazel and he called her Grandma Haze. At one point he needed additional surgery for a hernia that developed as a result of his constant crying from hunger. Miraculously, he pulled through, but Everett would have a long road to full recovery. Of course, I had no way of knowing this is what would happen and a lot of the time I had to rely on faith and determination.

As if things weren't difficult enough, the insurance company refused to pay the hospital and doctor bills. Because Everett was operated on when he was twenty-nine days old the insurance company managed to find a loophole having to do with a thirty-day time period. My husband's job brought in so little money and the burden of paying this bill fell to me. This is one of those horror stories about "fine print," so now I was saddled with a huge medical bill that would take the next seven years to pay off. But pay it off I did. With every check I mailed, I felt stronger and more empowered. This, I decided was just another exercise in growth.

Unfortunately, because of the scarcity of money, I was not able to stay home with my baby the way most other women in my community did. In fact, I was the only woman in my circle of friends who had to work and I resented it and felt cheated. Every morning when I dropped my baby off with Grandma, I put on a happy face and got in my car to drive to work. Before I could get out of the driveway the tears began to flow. On the ride to work I just cried and cried. By the time I arrived at the office I had to reapply my makeup. Each morning, I waited until I couldn't wait any longer and called Grandma to see how he was doing.

"Why, we are doing just fine. He is such a good baby," was her usual response.

"Now don't you fuss and worry we'll see you later." As I hung up the phone I realized what a gift I had given her. For the first time I realized that Grandma Haze needed that baby as much as we needed her. Since my sister Gerry was getting married soon Grandma Haze and Emmeretta would be alone and the arrival of this baby brought joy to that home. Grandma Haze would wait at the front door every morning to receive her bundle of joy. I saw the happiness in her eyes and heard the joy in her voice. Grandma Haze was happy and animated with stories about Everett.

"He found his toes today. He smiled. He clapped his hands," she would say. I could see the joy in her face. One day as I backed out of the driveway, after dropping Everett off, for the first time there were no tears. I had finally come to grips with leaving my baby with her. I accepted that it was a good thing to do. I believe caring for Everett gave new meaning to her life. She loved babies, especially this one. A few months later she would have her happiness doubled when her granddaughter Bonnie needed someone to watch her new baby, Tracy.

So while I was more than satisfied with the joys of motherhood, my married life continued with very little exuberance. It was as if my husband and I simply existed instead of being partners side by side. *This is not what I imagined it would be like.* Apart from the time I spent with my son, there was no fun, no enthusiasm, nothing. I buried those painful thoughts and feelings and went about the daily task of surviving. Our days were routine work, work and more work. After a long day we would have dinner without speaking a word to the other. Young Everett would be chatting about his day.

"So how was your day?" I would offer my husband.

"Miserable, what do you think?" He would respond.

I cherished the weekends when I had two uninterrupted days with my baby. We would play, read books and those days made life worth living and cancelled out all the negativity for me.

My marriage, not too solid to start with, was slowly falling apart. My husband was always complaining of not feeling well. We did not know then, as we do today, that he suffered from manic depressive disorder. Perhaps if we had been more aware, we could have sought the right help, the right medication. But at that time, no real help was available. Everett began to self-medicate with pills. He mixed uppers and downers with a bottle of scotch and hoped to numb his pain. Never having really identified the problem and simply refusing to face the fact that he *had* problems, he would begin to drink more and more.

There was nothing I could do and I knew it. I worked hard at trying to make our life appear normal to the outside world, for I did not want my child to feel *different*, as I had felt. Occasionally, I would suggest that Everett attend church with us or go to the carnival or maybe the park. He wanted no part of any of it he just wanted to be miserable. We would attend a party now and again or go to friends' houses for a house party. Back in the 60's our group of friends took turns going to each other's homes and listening to music and dancing. It was fun. I must say I did a pretty good job keeping up the happy marriage charade, but I might have served myself and my son better if I had been more concerned with getting better treatment for my family. My effort to make our life appear normal was my way of denying that conditions were rapidly deteriorating.

There is a price for everything, and I was beginning to pay the price of keeping up the charade of my life. By denying our problems, I allowed my body to create illness. How could it not? The emotions that needed to be expressed were not being honored and my body protested. I had one operation after another for a variety of maladies: thyroid disorder, ovarian cysts, lumps in my breast, exploratory procedures to investigate excessive weight loss. Then, most heartbreaking, I had a series of miscarriages. Both my body and mind were screaming messages: too much stress, too much living out of harmony with nature. Too much of my life was spent living in constant stress, worry and anxiety.

Through some aspects of my life were disintegrating I remained concerned about keeping up appearances. It was so very important to me to portray what I thought was a normal life for my son. I always wanted him to feel normal and accepted. One day, out of the blue, my mother called with an important news bulletin: she was coming up to my church to get married to my father.

"Are you crazy?" I asked. I was a grownup and I could finally tell her what I felt about things.

"Do you realize I have to *live* in this town? Do you have any idea how this will affect me and my family, living in a small town of Bible-carrying people?" There was silence on the other end of the phone.

"No way Mom!" I continued. She tried to explain away her thoughtless suggestion but I would not buy it.

"You find yourself a justice of the peace, have your wedding, and leave me out of it" I said. She did. I realized again what I had always known but never wanted to admit mom had no clue about anything, no idea about how her actions, past or present, would impact her children. Nor, did she really care.

A few weeks after my mother's nuptials, we took our son and dutifully made a trip to New York. We would be helping mother and her new husband celebrate this step in their lives and would also meet my father's grown son, Jack. It was an ill-conceived plan that seemed like a good idea (at least to me) at the time. But the day was headed for disaster.

To start with, my husband and my mother were like oil and water. Everett hated my mother and made no bones about it. My mother walked through life with a sense of entitlement and that really made him crazy. He knew her and much of her history of mothering and disliked her from the start. She also had very little use for him. She always told me I could have done much better. When my mother would come to visit he would leave and not return until she was gone. As I think back that was probably a good thing because there was much less stress. He typically avoided her and against my better judgment I talked him into going with me on this particular visit. I soon regretted that.

We arrived at my mother and father's apartment in Brooklyn, New York. A small one bedroom inundated with clutter. We all sat in the small living room waiting for the arrival of Jack and Barbara. But it wasn't long before the old hurt and resentments started to surface. In an effort to keep my husband placated, my mother offered him a scotch, then another and another. This was exactly what he did not need, but both my mother and Everett were unstoppable. If Everett had not been an alcoholic, he could have refused the additional drinks, but in a situation like this he was soon totally wasted.

When Jack and Barbara finally did arrive, all hell broke loose. My husband had fallen asleep on the couch. Little Everett, in the midst of playing, or maybe wanting attention, threw a pillow, hitting his father and waking him up. Quick to anger, my husband lunged and hit me. Dad and my newfound brother Jack rose to my defense. Jack, a big man, grabbed my husband and threw him on the couch. He threatened to throw him out the apartment window, telling him he was less than a man. He swore if he ever hit me again, he would come after him. I was crying hysterically and trying to comfort my son at the same time. My mother was trying to get my father in the other room while Jack's wife was pulling at him, telling him to stop. Not surprisingly, that was the end of our visit.

On our way home, we got very, very lost. But at least I had finally met my half brother, who I thought was a great guy and with whom I felt an instant connection. Too bad in the confusion and upset of the day, we didn't start a relationship. That would come years later.

Of course, the trouble in my marriage had not begun that day. It had always been there, always festering. I knew from the start that this marriage was not a good one and that my husband was not interested in making our life together work. I, like so many women in this situation, worked very hard at trying to make this union successful. Even though I was not happy, I so much wanted to create a good home for my son and a life that was not like the tattered, unpredictable and insecure one I had had as a child. I always made sure that discussions or arguments Everett and I had were never around our son. Wanting so much for little Everett to have something resembling a normal life, I never complained about anything around him. I just carried on as if life were wonderful. After all, it was not his fault that things turned out this way. I created this mess by not having the courage to leave this relationship as soon as I knew it was wrong. Why should a little boy have to suffer? But hard as I tried, nothing I did worked, and as the years passed, life just got worse. I was working harder and harder and my husband was working less and less. We were pulling in two different directions and had different goals. Perhaps he had no goals. I wanted so many things, and I wanted to make up for what had been lost earlier.

The day after the fiasco, my mother called to give me an earful about my husband. She refused to acknowledge her role of alcohol enabler.

As much as I was very aware my husband had big problems and that I was in an abusive situation, I still saw my mother as a contributor to this misery.

"You know, Mother, you have no right to talk" I began.

"Here you are with six kids. No one but me knows anything about their father. You have some nerve to sit in judgment of others." That was the end of that call. My words were instrumental, though, in bringing to light information that was long buried. A few days later, the rest of my siblings got a letter explaining the circumstances of their conception and who their fathers were. That was when we learned we were six siblings with five different fathers. Only Pauline and Jamie had the same father.

Four

About 15 years into my marriage, my husband had become a full-blown alcoholic. He was employed at a land surveyor's office as a draftsman and sometimes filled in for the field crew chief. He was good at what he did when he worked but he was working less and less and drinking more and more. He was a scotch drinker and it was nothing for him to down a quart every night. Everett called himself an 11 o'clock alcoholic. When he would arrive home from work he always complained about not feeling well. He rarely ate dinner with little Everett and me. He would sit in his chair watch television and about 9 p.m. he would mix his first drink. Two hours later, he'd head for his favorite bar. About 3 a.m. he arrived back home. I worried I would get a call from the local police telling me he had been arrested for another DWI or worse. As a result of this behavior very often he was unable to get up and go to work.

"Call me in," he would say from behind the covers on his side of the bed. This would happen a few times a week. Try as I might, I could not make him better. I did everything I could think of I would refuse to buy his scotch and continually begged him to join AA. I even tried to get him involved with the church. He continued to drink heavily and never showed remorse for what he did or how he treated his family. By this time I knew he would not change and that it was not my fault. I now had to figure out what I needed to do to make my life better for me and my son.

After years of dreaming about buying his ideal car, a Chevy Suburban with a 30-gallon gas tank, Everett bought one. It was the '70s then and the gas crunch made this type of car totally impractical. It seemed to me that when it came to wise choices, my ex just never got it right.

Making mistakes is not a crime, I know, but Everett never owned up to any of them. He believed his problems were always someone else's fault. Everett had already racked up three DWIs over the course of our marriage. I always bailed him out and bought him another car when he crashed the one he had. I take responsibility for my part in this portion of his life unfortunately he always promised to stop and I foolishly chose to believe him. I am just grateful he did not kill or maim himself or someone else. I was convinced his drinking and subsequent behavior was my fault, allowing those old feelings of rejection to cloud my thinking and not really seeing him for who he was. I was convinced I could make him a better father, husband and overall person however, I never could.

Of course, he was rarely rational enough to evaluate what was happening in his life. He spent time in and out of psychiatric hospitals, took all kinds of pills, tranquilizers, anti-depressants, and never stopped drinking. Somehow in that twisted state he kept thinking he would find a cure for his woes. He was depressed all the time and walked with constant pain both emotionally and physically. Everett also believed that the pain had nothing to do with his lifestyle and behavior. Everett continued to look for that pill that would make his demons go away. The first time I checked him into the hospital it was gut wrenching on all levels. What do I tell people, I wondered? What would I tell my son? His parents? I cried the first time I admitted him.

What a failure I was as a wife. When I arrived home I sat in the driveway for a long time, thinking I should just go pick up my son, get our things and keep on driving to where I had no idea. But I was no quitter I would get out of the car, go into the house and figure out what we do when he comes home. After all maybe they would finally fix him.

After all these people were professionals. They could deal with addicts and my husband was an addict. I had to face it.

Yet there was no improvement, not even after his hospitalization. He had had drugs, electroshock therapy and much, much more, but nothing made him better. I will say it was not the hospitals fault. Everett refused their instructions and help. It would be years later after he would lose everything that he would join Alcoholics Anonymous, which saved him. As of this writing, he has been clean and sober for about 15 years. I am so pleased, most of all for my son. My son was the one who bore the brunt of care for his father after we left.

But that was then. Before that sobriety difficult times would prevail. When the violence began, I wondered as most battered women do, what have I done to make him so angry? When I would confront him about coming home yanking me out of bed and blaming me for everything that was wrong in his life, he would throw me against the wall, slap me around a bit and then usually collapse into a drunken sleep. Everett was a pro at forgetting. I know now that an alcohol blackout means you don't remember anything from the night before. His drinking had put him into an altered state and he really didn't remember what had happened. But that didn't matter. The violence progressed. First it was just his hands, then fists, then knives. My life at this time was very difficult, especially since I was trying to put on a happy face for my son and the world. Not only was I trying to have a career and give my son a normal life I was struggling with this nightmare at home. I often called it my after-dark life. When the sun shown, life was good but when the sun went down my life turned into a nightmare. I remember one cold winter night the front door swung open and he stumbled in.

"I'm home," he yelled.

"Get the hell out of that bed and fix me some eggs to eat."

I jumped out of bed, found my slippers and ran to the cold kitchen, franticly grabbing for the frying pan to make him his eggs. Not wanting to incite another confrontation I dutifully made the eggs without complaint. It was then, standing at the stove making him eggs and bacon when I felt the cold barrel of the gun at my temple. He had been target shooting the day before and I could smell the gunpowder. The smell of the metal barrel and the gunpowder were so strong it made me nauseous and I truly believed I was going to die. The violence and sadistic behavior had never gone this far. How had I let it get this far?

"Them dam eggs better be good or I'll use this on you." I heard him move over and pull the kitchen chair out from the table.

"You know it's always loaded and I can make it look like an accident."

"Not to worry, these eggs will be the best ever," I said serving him his food. I began to perspire and shake uncontrollably. I was waiting for him to tell me I could go back to bed.

He glared at me.

"What the hell's wrong with you? Get out of here get out of my sight."

In that moment my life did flash before me I knew I had to go. There would be no turning back this time. As I look back I am still amazed I stayed so long. I guess somehow I figured it was my fault. I wasn't pretty enough, thin enough or maybe I was a disappointment as a wife and mother. I never recognized that my husband had an illness. And in a way so did I. Again, I let my feelings of unworthiness blind me to who he really was.

The night he held a gun to my head I thought it would be easier if he pulled the trigger however, I knew I needed to be there for my son so I ran out of the kitchen and back to the bedroom. The next thing I heard was the car starting and he was on his way back to his favorite bar. After all his drinking buddies and favorite bartender understood him! That night I knew it was up to me to put an end to this way of life.

After he drove off I went upstairs and slept in my son's room. Fortunately he was at his girlfriend's house and would not be back until after school the next day. I was comforted with the fact that he was now sixteen and spent much time away from home. The next morning when I got up to go to work, I tiptoed into my room to get my clothes. Everett rolled over and told me to call his boss.

"Tell him I am sick and can't come to work," he said. I walked to the phone and dialed his office. When his boss answered I identified myself.

"My husband is drunk again and can't come to work today." I glanced over at him. I could see the fury in his eyes as he jumped out of the bed and headed towards me, screaming I was a waste of human flesh. I quickly hung up the phone and ran for the door.

"You get back here I'm not finished with you." I was already down the stairs through the garage and into my car. I knew that was it for me. I always did what he asked for fear of his retaliation. I lived my life trying to keep confrontation to a minimum. I knew he would slap the daylights out of me as he had done in the past, if he caught me. The one thing I am so grateful for is that miraculously my son was rarely around when his father was out of control. That's not to say he never saw him drunk. He did and I remember one night he came running downstairs when he heard his father slapping me around and punched him and pulled him away from me. I find it difficult to forgive myself for not protecting him from a scene like that. Sometimes as I lay awake and sleep won't come, I wonder how I came to have this life. All I wanted was to have a home, be a good wife and mom. Somehow that didn't seem to be in the cards for me. I was also sure that if I did not make some changes for me and my son it never would be.

That night I went to the home of my coworker, Cathy, who lived in a new apartment complex in a nearby town. We ate dinner and then strolled around the grounds.

"This is a place where I could live," I said to myself. The next day I inquired with the super about available apartments and learned that there was only one left on the ground floor. I asked him to reserve it for me and promised to come by after work to see it.

I had originally thought that I wanted a ground floor apartment, but with more thought, I realized that I was alone much of the time; and maybe a second floor place would be better. But since there was just one vacant apartment, I would have to take whatever I could get. I was use to that.

The super greeted me in the parking lot and explained the circumstances.

"I know that you want a ground floor but the only one that is left is on the second floor", he said.

A sign. A wish fulfilled. I was thrilled.

"No problem," I said, but I was thinking. It's mine! I knew I was doing the right thing.

When I arrived home that night, my husband wanted to talk. He promised for the umpteenth time that he would stop drinking and go for help.

"I swear to you Joanne I will go back to the shrink and do that counseling thing."

"It's too late," I said.

"I have made other plans." He had heard this so many times I was sure he did not believe me.

"Sorry pal, I have it all worked out and there is no turning back for me. This time it's the real thing. Everett will be living with me."

He stood up and walked over to me, his arms stretched out his face beat red and shaking.

"Oh please, give me just one more chance, I promise I will get into counseling and even join AA if you will stay." I thought of the other evening, the gun held to my head. I stood my ground.

"Everett, how many times have I heard that same song and dance, no this time I am going and please do not call me, I am having the office screen my calls."

"No, no, please stay, just one more chance I will really work at it this time."

"Well, how about this? You get sober and then we can talk." He pleaded with me and then began to cry and I am ashamed to say I didn't care. That was usually the point when I caved; not this time. I went to bed. As usual he, went out, got drunk and smashed up another vehicle. This type of behavior kept us in continuous debt, sometimes I felt I worked just to keep him in cars. This kind of chaos had become too much for me. I had lived with it growing up and knew the time was drawing near to have a different kind of life.

The next morning, as we were both getting ready for work, I noticed a piece of paper sticking out of my husband's jacket pocket. He was out of the room and I could not resist. I pulled out the slip of paper and unfolded it. A love letter, that's what it was. A love letter from one of his lady friends. It was poorly spelled, badly written, but what a perfect piece of incriminating evidence. Evidently she had met my son and was now remarking on what a lovely young man he was!

"What a great job you've done raising your boy," she wrote in her sorry note. Sorry, deluded woman. There were little jokes about me playing right into their plan so they could get together that night. *What a fool she is*, I thought. *A poor uneducated fool.*

At this point we had been married almost 20 years. There were a few years before the drinking started that were, I thought at the time, good enough for me. Looking back, I realize my dreams were meager ones. I always felt I would be lucky if someone married me and I could have a child. This I thought would make me whole. My dream of wholeness was soon just that, a dream. Our life was simply about existing day to day, and I felt my job was to make it as normal a life for my son as I could. He was a good kid. For the most part, I was able to shield him from the behavior of his father. Since my husband was an after 11 alcoholic, the good part of that was that my son was usually asleep and did not have to witness this side of his father. Everett knew his father was an alcoholic; however, I am ashamed to say we never talked about it. As I think back, it was almost like the old saying, see no evil, hear no evil, do no evil. I know now that was not the way to handle the situation, but it worked for us at the time. As my son got older his father would take him to the local pub to play pool. I soon realized this was done so my husband would have a ride home. I quickly put a stop to that when I realized what was going on.

It was about midnight when Everett drove in the driveway with his dad. They came in and I told Everett to get to bed, reminding him the bus came at 7 AM. As my son climbed the stairs to his bedroom, I turned to his father and told him his son was not his personal driver and his rest was far more important than his pool game. One of my greatest regrets is not being honest with my son, of pretending our life was normal when it was not. Although I thought at the time he was not affected by the things he did manage to witness I was wrong. How could he not have been affected? I am sure through his adult life that what he did witness has crept into his life on occasion. My son is a good husband and dad. I think at some point he realized he was drinking a bit too much and unlike his father, recognized it and put a stop to that behavior. I am not saying he doesn't have an occasional beer however I am saying he is determined not to follow in the footsteps of his father.

On the morning when I finally left, my husband for good he found me with his lover's note and lunged at me but I drew my hand back quickly. He knew I had read it so it was too late. He just stood there and said nothing, not even, "I'm sorry."

I was relieved. I had been planning to leave, but now I had a note from a girlfriend, which really helped erase any doubt I may have had. Not only was I married to an alcoholic but also a cheater.

"For heaven's sake," I said, "She can't even spell!" What could he say? To this day, I still have that note. On occasion I come across it and pause to re-read it. I am always amazed at how happy it makes me feel. It was my ticket to freedom, without guilt.

Because I had had so many false starts, at leaving, my husband never believed that I really would do it. I was like the boy who cried wolf. Each time I would threaten to leave he would manage to convince me he would get help and I would cave and give him another chance. Certainly now that I had confirmation that there were other women which I had suspected, but could never prove. I had forgiven him so many times and hoped he would change and now I knew that there would be no change. Thinking about the night before and the incident with the gun I realized it was me who had to make the change, and this time I was ready. When he finally understood that I was not bluffing, that I really was leaving, things got uglier than ever.

It was Saturday. My in-laws were not aware of the problems we were having and had no idea I was about to leave. After Everett's father retired, they split their time between Massachusetts and Florida and had no clue about what was going on in our lives. By then I had adopted a philosophy of not speaking about my problems until I was ready to do something about them. No one knew what went on in my life, not even my sister or my closest friends. I suggested that my husband take a ride to see his parents. It was only fair to let them know what was going on. Grudgingly, he agreed, and left the house. That's when I gathered up my personal items, loaded my car, and drove to my new apartment. Upon returning to pick up another load, exhaustion overcame me, and I made the mistake of lying down for a nap.

That's when Everett returned. On his way home from his parent's house, he stopped at his favorite bar. Now equipped with the false sense of confidence that comes from liquor, he was primed for a confrontation. He woke me and started a tirade, trying to convince me to change my mind about leaving. But he couldn't convince me and so he got angrier and then violent. He began to scream obscenities at me.

"You won't last a day by yourself." He smashed another hole in the wall. I stood there watching him destroy the house he and his father had built.

"You will come crawling back in no time," he said. I have to say, the statement made me reflect for a moment. Could I really do this on my own? Then came my light bulb moment. What had I been doing for the past 20 years? I knew I could do it. By then I had started to pack the last of my things. I had boxes all over the bedroom floor and was quickly filling them with my personal belongs. Nothing else mattered. I certainly did not want to bring anything that would remind me of my life with him. I grabbed the essentials: some utensils, a few plates, cups, glasses and my favorite pots, just enough to get me through until I had time to settle in. Oh yes, the baby picture frame with my son's first pair of shoes. I had them bronzed. I must not forget that. It was very sad. I had so many dreams of being the perfect wife and mom and now I was thinking that I wasn't much better than my own mother. I had failed just as she did.

As my husband ranted around the house, he started dumping the boxes and throwing the stuff all over. I calmly walked around and picked up the things and placed them back in the boxes. I thought of how pathetic we were the two of us and that I couldn't wait to get out of this place. He screamed and smashed while I packed.

Comically, in the middle of all this, his mother called.

"I am calling to beg you. You can't leave Everett!" You would think I was walking out on her. As her son continued his rage, I held the phone so she could hear.

"You tell me you love me like a daughter, so I want to know is this the way you want your daughter to live?" There was silence on the other end of the phone.

"This is how my life has been for a long, long time." Still no response.

"I deserve better," I told her. Everett seemed not to be listening, but stood examining the contents of a carton, a box of sweaters that had been packed away in the basement.

"I will pray for both of you," she said finally and hung up. Some glass broke behind me, my husband grabbed me, threw me against the wall.

'I'll give you one more chance to change your mind," he said.

"Or I will call my girlfriend!"

"Call her! Call her!" I screamed, and then watched as he stormed out of the house. Fearing he would return, I called my son, who was at his girlfriend's house and told him to stay there, since I was not sure what his father might do. I then called my best friend, Nicki, and went to her house for the night. I left and promised myself never to look back.

Five

Moving day arrived, and although many people had offered to help with the move, no one was around. That didn't stop me. I borrowed my friend's truck and my son and I loaded the remainder of our clothes and his things and my bedroom furniture into the vehicle. I told my 17 year-old son we were headed for our new life. As we drove towards our new home you could cut the tension with a knife.

"So tell me Everett what you are thinking right now." He didn't even look at me, just stared at his sneakers

"I'm thinking you have really messed up my life this time."

"What would you have me do, stay and continue to live a lie, not just me but you too?" He was fighting back tears but then caught himself. He turned and stared straight ahead.

"You never asked me what I wanted to do" he said.

"Like my opinion didn't matter it was all about you and dad." He was right and I felt awful I never did ask him. I just did what I had always done and did what I thought was best for the both of us. I forgot he was a young man and not a little boy and had the right to express his thoughts. But I was so busy trying to survive I forgot that.

"You know mom, I don't want to change schools. I only have one year left."

I stared at the road ahead.

"I understand and I have taken care of that. I got permission from the principal for you to finish out this year and next year and graduate with your friends. Oh and by the way, I will give you my car so you can get yourself back and forth with not having to wait on my work

73

schedule." He was delighted and certainly his mood changed and we got through that first day just fine. I still would need to attend to the sale of the house and was concerned that my husband might do something destructive to the house, but I couldn't think about that at this moment. I just had to get out and get to a safe place. At that very moment, I didn't care where he went or what he would do. Eventually he would relocate to Woodstock, NY.

Our two-bedroom apartment had a tiny kitchen and a dining area around the corner and oh such a cozy living room with a deck that faced the woods that was all mine! I knew there would be no way to pay both rent and a mortgage. It was imperative to sell that house. I had posted a note in the cafeteria at work listing the house. One of my co-workers who happened to live two doors up from me told me her daughter was looking to relocate to the area.

"Well Ruth, here's the deal, I need to unload this house ASAP, if your daughter is serious I will give her a fair price."

She looked around the house checking the kitchen and bath.

"You bet she is serious we will stop back tonight after work and she can take a look." Amazingly, her daughter took one look at the house and said right then that she would buy it. Knowing I would get resistance from my husband. I enlisted the help of his father, a man of few words and would always take the road to less confrontation. He knew I was determined and I believe knew it was over for me and his son. His parents had given us the property to build our house on; however, the paperwork was never done to remove his father's name from the deed. I asked his father to sign off on the deed to only me. This would allow me to sell the house without my husband's signature. Sign he did, and I sold the house. Everett was not happy about the sale of the house, however after the sale took place, he was happy to receive half the profits.

The easy sale of the house had been the first lucky thing that had happened to me in a long time. I took this as another confirmation that I was doing the right thing. I would always need this kind of encouragement by random signs, since I never had had a voice in any decisions about my life. It would be a long, long time until I would trust myself and the choices I was beginning to make. In the meantime, I relied on these little incidents to confirm that I was pointed in the right direction.

I moved into my new space with only bedroom furniture and no money. My son chose to stay with his father until the house sold and then came to live with me in our new apartment. My son's girlfriend, Debbie lived just minutes away and he spent the majority of his time at her home. He was also attending school and the commute was much shorter than it would be when he lived with me. Then another stroke of luck happened. Unexpectedly, my employer decided to give us a mid-year bonus. This had never been done before and for me it was a godsend. Receiving this bonus when I was flat broke was another sign for me that I had done the right thing. I went home to my new apartment and danced around the empty rooms knowing this bonus would help me fill the place with furniture to make a cozy home. This turn of events made me feel empowered and ready to take on the world. I was grateful that things were finally going well. Now that I had a new place to live and had sold the house, I took the next step and filed for divorce. My new life was underway and for the first time ever I was calling the shots. It was a new sensation for me and I liked it.

I spent the rest of the summer decorating my new home with the help of my friend Nicki. I never had a say about anything before, so making a decision about the color of the drapes or type of light fixture in the dining room was difficult.

"No problem" Nicki said. She was more than willing to make those decisions with me. To this day, she is a woman with an amazing sense of style and just instinctively knows what works. On shopping trips we spent days going store to store to make my new home as warm and tasteful as possible. During those shopping trips we spent hours talking about my situation and she was a constant source of support and strength. Before this I always doubted myself and the choices I had made in life. Nicki would have none of that kind of talk. She was truly my strength during this difficult time. Although Nicki had long suspected my marriage was in trouble she never said a word. I was always telling her things were fine I was not willing to talk about my troubles until I was ready to do something about them and she instinctively knew that.

How wonderful it was to go to bed at night and not worry about getting a call from the police telling me that my husband had been arrested for drunk driving, yet another time. It was so comforting to know that I could sleep without the fear of an inebriated husband coming home to rant and rave and smack me around. I was slowly learning that life could be good. I was also learning that I could be on my own, care for my son's needs, handle my career and even make good decisions about all of this. I was not that person my husband tried to convince me I was. I was not helpless and not weak and most of all I was a good person.

It was at this time that my brother Jack called me and asked me to meet him in Westchester. We met at a local restaurant and when I arrived, I barely recognized him. We had not seen each other since the death of our father ten years earlier. He looked much older now, more strained. I wondered if my life experiences were beginning to show on me. Did I also look older? I was sure I did. As we talked, he told me that he had met someone and had left his wife, Barbara. He felt that he was searching for something, but he did not know what that something was. I asked him if the fact that our father had stayed with his mother, even though he didn't love her if this added to his confusion. We were sitting in a dimly lit corner of the restaurant Jack looked at me for a long time then took a sip of his beer.

"You know I hated your mother for so long," he said.

"I blamed her for dad leaving my mom. I now know that she was not the problem, it was them. I am now sorry he took so long to leave."

I looked across the table at him.

"I know Jack but they were all about them and did not really care about the feelings of your mother or us."

Jack dropped his head and wiped his brow.

"I remember when my mom and our dad were married, she couldn't wait to sign the support checks and send them to your mom. I think that sums it up, don't you?"

"Yea, I guess it does," he said. Unfortunately, as their only child, Jack was left to deal with the backlash of his father leaving. As the two of us talked and sipped our drinks I had the impression Jack was disillusioned with life in general. I felt bad for him. I gave him what I thought was the only good advice. I assured him he had to follow his heart. When he told me he wanted me to meet this new woman in his life, I agreed, just to confirm my support.

During that summer, Jack and I saw quite a bit of each other. He apologized for not having contacted me sooner, but explained after the ugly scene in mom's apartment, he had no use for my husband and did not want to be anywhere near him. I thought this was our opportunity to make up for lost time, and several years later we spent a week together in the Bahamas. It seemed then that he was still struggling and wrestling with many decisions. He had gone back to his wife Barbara, but did not seem at peace with that decision.

Over time, Jack and Barbara seemed to have worked out some of their differences. Then in August 2002 Barbara left a message on my machine telling me that Jack had died. I was stunned. I had spoken to him a few weeks earlier and he had made no mention of how ill he was. I didn't know that he was dying of cirrhosis of the liver. I only knew in his younger days he had been a heavy drinker but I had no idea this was still the case. We saw each other infrequently and I never witnessed that side of him. I felt somewhat cheated that I was not privy to this information. At Jack's memorial service his wife told me that he would not want me to see him that way. I didn't buy it. I would have appreciated the opportunity of saying goodbye to my brother, of telling him that I loved him. His friends had the chance and yet I, his only sibling, did not. I will always feel sad about that and when that sadness hits me, I whisper a small prayer – *Jack, I love you and I miss you!*

In my newly-constructed life, I spent most of my time at home alone, but I did not mind. The peace and quiet was a novelty. Although I enjoyed my newfound solitude, a part of me knew my son was somewhat upset with me and understandably so. Although Everett III officially lived with me, he spent the majority of his time with his girlfriend, Debbie, a cute girl with beautiful blond hair. He felt that I had turned our lives upside down and that I had taken him away from the neighborhood he knew. All of this was true. Children can rarely understand why parents make the moves they make. When I was young I had to accept my mother's moves and ideas that changed my life. I had no say in what happened to me. I didn't want my son to feel that way and tried to convey to him what I had done was best both for him and for me. We needed to get out of that town because that was where my now ex-husband had grown up. I did not want to be part of that context. I wanted something new, something fresh.

Now that he was 17, Everett was driving his own car and commuting to school. This was his last year of high school and he was looking forward to graduating in June. So his own life was shaping up as he was approaching adulthood. During the week he would stay at Debbie's house and on weekends he and Debbie would spend time with my ex-husband. I do believe Everett and Debbie did help his father get on his feet. Debbie would cook meals for him and tidy the apartment. I also think when they were around, Everett's father drank less. It would be years before his father would finally join AA and begin to turn his life around. It was during this time that my son and I lost some of the closeness we had always had when he was younger. It was a necessary step in his growth though, as he had to form his own ideas and make his own choices. He did continue with his life after gradation he worked towards making a life for himself. In fact, he has gone on to become a wonderful young man a terrific husband and father of two beautiful girls, Lauren and Katherine. A person of good character my son is community-minded and treats everyone, including himself, with respect. I am very proud of him and grateful for the way he turned out. He had survived some terrible, life-threatening circumstances as a baby, but life was given back to him. He had to make the best of his circumstances as a child and teenager. Not everyone can do that, and I acknowledge him for his accomplishments. It was hard to see back then how it would all turn out, but in spite of it all, we did all right!

The summer passed and we were headed towards fall. I was feeling quite comfortable enjoying my new grown-up status. This was the first time I felt in control of my life, the first time I knew I was powerful and could change the course of things. I would no longer be stuck with decisions that no longer suited me. Although the majority of the time I *lived* by myself since my son spent most of his time at Debbie's house, I had a wonderful support system of family, friends and co-workers. Some of my friends were single and had active social lives, but I wanted no part of it. I was very happy just being me and living my life without tears, fear and turmoil. The absence of pain was peace, I discovered, and peace had been a pretty rare commodity throughout my life.

One day a friend suggested a blind date with a fellow her husband worked with. I told her I would think about it and it took me about three or four months to finally agree to let her give this man my phone number. I suppose he was a bit hesitant too, because it took him several weeks to call. When he did, though, we talked for a very long time, which was encouraging for each of us.

On the phone, I learned that Joe seemed like a nice guy, was divorced with two kids, a daughter Kerry 12 and John 14. Joe's son John lived with him and he had his daughter every other weekend. Kerry would eventually come to live with Joe fulltime. He was also caring for his mother, Ann. Quite a package children, a household to run and a mom. I figured he had to be a person of good character to have that level of responsibility. Still, he made room for me, and we marked our calendars for a date on the Friday after Thanksgiving, 1981.

On the day of our blind date, I had an uneasy feeling. I had not dated in a long time and felt unsure about the whole plan. I was thirty-eight years old, had been married for almost twenty years and had never had a serious relationship other than with Norman and with my ex-husband. Now it was the '80s and I was sure that everything had changed since my dating days of the late '50s and early '60s. Still, I decided not to think about the blind date horror stories I'd heard and got ready for my date with Joe. It took me hours to get ready. At least an hour was devoted to hair and make-up. Then the painful decision, what to wear. After several calls to Nicki it was decided I would wear a pair of designer jeans and a green velour top.

Joe had some mix-ups with arrangements for babysitting that night, and we nearly had to postpone our plans but he worked it out and showed up. When the doorbell rang, I broke out in the same cold sweat one does at sixteen and when I saw Joe I felt the same surge of delight one feels at sixteen. He stood there, six foot six. I'd always dreamed of being with a tall, tall man, because at five foot seven, I towered over most guys. I invited Joe in and, excusing myself for a moment, ran and changed into high heels. It was rare that I could wear them and still be the shorter person in the couple!

I offered Joe a glass of wine and we sat and talked; I was trying not to let my anxiety show. After a brief chat, we realized it was getting late and we left to meet Flip and Art, the friends who had set up this date.

By the time we arrived at the restaurant Flip and Art were waiting for us. As we apologized for being late, Joe pulled my chair out at the table. I couldn't remember the last time a man had done that for me.

"I'm thinking lamb," I said as we flipped through the menu. Then I realized I should order something inexpensive; it was our first date and he would probably grab the check.

"I'm thinking duck," Joe said. Flip and Art grunted across the table.

"Duck yes" I smiled. We spent a pleasant evening at the restaurant of the local ski lodge. As we ate dinner we watched the skiers on the slopes. There was a fire blazing and sputtering in the fireplace and the lighting was just perfect for the occasion. And there we sat, talking, laughing and just feeling good. It was relaxing and encouraging being with other people this way. Afterward, we headed over to Flip and Art's for drinks.

Later, Joe took me home and I invited him in for coffee. The last time I invited someone in for coffee it was a disaster. He thought it was an invitation for the rest of the evening. I quickly showed him the front door and that was the last of him. What was I thinking? But Joe was different. I trusted him and had a feeling it would be okay. We drank several pots of coffee that night. Like many good friendships, this one began with a conversation that did not end for hours. We seemed to agree on many ideas, especially on our ideas on marriage. We had both been hurt badly and did not want to remarry. Anyway, that was how is seemed that night.

We talked all through the night and into the morning. I had planned to go Christmas shopping with Gerry and my niece, Yvonne, and Joe was still at my place when they arrived. Gerry quickly retreated and said she would be back in an hour. Joe and I said our goodbyes. He held me for a long time and then kissed me goodbye. He was then on his way to get his kids. I wondered if I would ever see him again. I felt I had a new best friend.

Within moments of Joe's leaving Gerry and Yvonne arrived and we were off to the mall. Although we were all set to do some real shopping, we didn't get much done. The girls were more interested in hearing about my blind date. We found a coffee shop and sat and talked.

"How was it?" Gerry asked with excitement.

"Tell us everything!" Yvonne said.

"This guy." I smiled across the table at them.

"Now this is the kind of guy I could spend the rest of my life with." I felt like the Cheshire cat. They wanted details so I told them how we talked more that night than I had during my entire marriage to my ex-husband.

On Sunday night Joe called to tell me what a great time he had and to ask for another date. I was on cloud nine, just like a teenager. He was too good to be true tall, good-looking, kind, sensitive and funny and he actually called back. The whole thing was almost too good to be true, I knew. I was told by very wise friends in the dating arena this kind of thing rarely happened.

We fell into a routine. Joe had his kids, John and Kerry, every other weekend and we began to see each other alternate weekends. That was perfect, for it allowed us to move slowly and think about what we were doing. We had both come out of difficult marriages and wanted to avoid the same mistakes. We both had busy and demanding careers and families and friends to which we were committed. Joe was a guidance counselor at George Fischer Middle School and I was an operations manager at the Foundation for Christian Living. Yet, somehow we made room in our lives for each other.

When I started dating Joe, he was all I needed and I promptly dropped out of circulation. Not to imply I had ever really been in circulation. Before I met Joe I had a couple of dates, one with a doctor, who made it very clear that he needed to bring home a nice Jewish girl to have his children. Well this Irish gal did not fit the description. My next date, set up by a friend, was with a guy who owned a trucking company. That was a disaster; I practically had to throw him out of my apartment. Then there was the fuel delivery guy. He arrived at my apartment and immediately announced we were going to the pizza place and I could order anything on the menu because he had taken $100 out of the bank for our date. Oh boy, now what do I do? Always wanting to please, we went to the pizza place where the most expensive thing on the menu was $6. As our date ended, rather early, he mentioned that he was not really divorced but was working on it. He asked if he could call again and I told him I did not date married men. I was batting zero in the dating game. Then I met Joe. We dated for five years and in that time;

life was quite dramatic. Within the first year of our relationship, I was diagnosed with breast cancer. This, I thought, would send any sensible man running. Who would want that kind of responsibility, that worry? But that's not what happened. On the contrary, Joe stayed right by my side and has been by my side ever since.

Pauline, John, Gerry and Me in front of the children's center on one of mom's rare visits.

Gerry, John, me, Pauline and Jamie in front on Jamie's visit to our foster home 1953.

Our Foster Home 1952

Gerry, Bonnie, me and Pauline on Easter Sunday 1952

My foster parents in 1957.

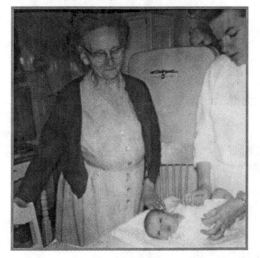

Me changing Everett for his first doctor visit.
My foster mother looking on 1964.

My foster mother holding Everett and my mother looking on 1964.

My father and Everett 1965.

My mother and father early 1970's.

Me, Joe, Kerry and Joe's mom Ann. Celebrating her birthday in the mid 80s.

Everett giving me away at my wedding 1988

Joe and me 1988

Kerry, Joe, me and John at our wedding 1988.

Dr. Roth, my surgeon

My friend Nicki.

Friends and family at our family reunion 1990.

First time all my mother's children were together.
Photo from our family reunion 1990.

Our children, spouses, Joe and me and our
granddaughter Lauren at Kerry's wedding 1999.

Dr. Norman Vincent Peale with me at my retirement from the Peale Center in 1992.

My half brother Jack Keane with me in the early 1990's

Joe and me with our six grandchildren.

Six

It was a beautiful Saturday morning and on the surface, everything seemed right with the world. I had just returned from the post office where I picked up my final divorce papers. My ex and I had been divorced for a year by the time they arrived. During the course of the day I spent much time reflecting on my old life and everything I had done to try and make that marriage work. I had to trick my ex-husband into signing the divorce papers, tell him he would have to wine and dine me all over again and then we would see where it went. However, I knew I had no intention of rekindling anything with Everett. My ex signed the papers and I breathed a sigh of relief. I was free.

As of that day and for the first time in my life I was truly in charge of *me*. I did not have to do anything I did not want to do. What a novel concept. What a relief! I reflected on my 20 years of married life and wondered how I got through them. And before that, my life in the foster care system, where it was reinforced that I was less than worthy and should be grateful for whatever I had. I bought that idea for a very long time. How could I not? Several months before I left my husband I looked in the mirror and for a split second, I thought I saw the image of a very old, angry lady. I quickly shook myself and decided that would not be me. From that day forward I knew change was in my future.

I needed to do a lot of searching, to reach inside to a place I had long protected; to know what my needs were. From that day forward, I worked very hard at liking and taking care of myself. It's a good thing

I did all that preparing; because life was about to offer me more hard decisions to make.

One spring day, I received an invitation to attend my 20th class reunion. I considered going, then not going. I didn't much care for most of those people when I was in school. Why would I now pay to have dinner with them?

Since my social life was still a bit lacking I decided to check it out. I couldn't help but notice when I got there and looked around the room; time had caught up with the guys who had been very popular in high school. At my tenth high school reunion, I was acknowledged for having been married the longest. Now at my 20th I was the most recently divorced, not exactly an honor I was proud to receive but it was very freeing. At first I was self conscience about attending alone, but once there I was amazed at how the popular guys, who wouldn't give me a second look in high school, were now surrounding me as if I were the only single gal in town. How perspectives change with each decade! Apart from this realization, the night consisted of mainly small talk about kids, jobs, and failed relationships. When I got home I called Joe and reviewed the evening. By that time we had been dating for about 10 months. I told him I was the hot commodity among the single guys of the evening. He told me he was not surprised.

"If I had been there I would have approached you and worked my best smooth talk on you," he said. Then he went on to tell me how attractive, bright and funny I was.

"What a package!" he said. That kind of positive feedback was something I was not use to and I must say it made me feel so very worthy, something I rarely felt.

On Monday I went to the doctor for my annual gynecological check-up. As usual, he spent a lot of time palpating my cystic breasts, pausing on a particular spot in my left breast.

"You can sit up," he said, bending over to write on my chart. I pulled my gown closed. He looked up at me.

"I want to do a biopsy."

"Really, you mean…." Could it be that I had finally gotten my life together and now I was going to die from cancer? I was devastated.

"We just want to be sure." He headed toward the door.

"My nurse will schedule one for you. It was a pleasure," He extended his hand and I shook it. I'd had these lumps before, and they were always benign, but this time the doctor insisted I have it aspirated.

The doctor who tried to do a needle aspiration was unable to extract any fluid from the cyst. It was decided I would be admitted to the hospital for a surgical biopsy. At this point I was beginning to get a little nervous. I put on my usual brave face but inside I was so frightened. My thoughts wandered to dark places and I tried to rid myself of those thoughts but I could not.

Still, the day of the biopsy, I decided to have a positive attitude about the whole thing.

It was a beautiful fall day, crisp and sunny. The sun was shining brightly when Gerry picked me up for what was supposed to be one-day surgery. Gerry was cheery and full of chatter as I got into the car. She gave be a kiss and we were on our way. During the ride, we talked about the kids and Joe. Not a word was said about what was going to be the highlight of my day. Having been through this procedure already, I truly thought I would be just fine. I entered the hospital with a clear head and not a worry in the world. My name was called and Gerry gave me a hug and I was on my way.

The medical staff prepared for the procedure. I watched as the nurse hooked up the IV next to me. I would be alright, I told myself. I would be fine. I had to be. As the medical staff proceeded, they gave me some drugs to help me relax. I chatted and waited for the nurse to come and wheel me into the operating room. I suppose I should have been nervous, but I was rather optimistic about the outcome. After all, my life had really started to take a turn for the best. I was on a roll.

When I awoke, I checked the clock. The surgery had taken longer than expected. Sitting in my room, I waited for the doctor to come and give me the results. The bandages seemed to be unusually thick and not what I had experienced in the past. Usually there was just a small band-aid type cover over the incision. The mere fact that I was experiencing something different frightened me. I was a creature of habit and change was not easy for me to accept. I expected to be discharged. But I was uncomfortable and concerned about the pain. If they were simply removing a small lump, why was the pain so intense? In the past when this was done, I did not have this type of pain.

As the afternoon wore on and the doctor had not arrived, I started to grow anxious. Gerry tried to reassure me that the doctor was probably very busy and not to make a big deal out of it. I wondered about the longer than anticipated surgery. *Had there been a problem?* The doctor finally arrived. He put his hands behind him and backed up against the wall, as if he were holding it up.

"There is no easy way to tell you this. You have breast cancer. Surly I misunderstood him. *Breast cancer.* I began to perspire and I felt my throat tighten.

"It is a very fast-moving cancer," he continued. I am going to keep you here over the weekend and I will perform a mastectomy on Monday."

"Is there no other option for me?" My mind was racing. Oh my God. I was just starting to pull it together and now this. My head was spinning and I could barely stay focused enough to hear him.

"No," he said.

"The cancer has grown very fast and I suspect there is more."

"No" I screamed.

"Please be wrong, please go back to the lab and check the results again." I suppose doctors are used to this kind of reaction. I calmed down a bit. I thought about the day I made the appointment. Everything was *not* right with the world, after all, at least not with *my* world.

I must have blanked out somewhat after hearing I had cancer because my sister had to fill me in on the rest of the details. Gerry called Joe and told him she thought it would be good if he came over. She then lost her voice. I believe the circumstances of what had happened was extremely difficult for her, and she could not speak about it. When she arrived home she told her husband Bob and he had to make the calls to the family. I think that she experienced hysterical laryngitis. I had been anointed the family matriarch, the mother, the rock. If I were not around, to whom would Gerry turn? Like many women, I immediately began to blame myself for this. I wasn't sure how this was my fault but I was convinced that it was. Then I met the surgeon who put things into perspective.

"Let me tell you about yourself," he said. He stood there, a serious almost pompous look on his face. You are a woman who has a demanding job and a full personal life," he began.

"You take care of everyone else at your own expense and I am sure this has been going on for a very long time."

Maybe he was psychic, but then I realized that these doctors see many women like me all the time. I guess I fit the profile of sorts. Was I the typical cancer patient? Although I had told him nothing about myself or my life, he pegged me correctly. I was very willing to take responsibility for causing my cancer. I hadn't got much else right so far, why not? When I recall that conversation today, I can't believe I was so complacent and accepting of his statement. If indeed this was true, then I was angry at having a hand in creating this illness. But now I would go forward. I would take care of me!

It was a very long and tiring weekend. My hospital room was filled with friends who came to visit and encourage me, telling me that everything would be okay. I wondered how they could know that, but I guess people just don't know what to say. I was not confident that everything would be okay but I did know this: my life was about to change in more ways than one.

My son arrived looking pale, as if he had seen a ghost. He walked across the room, threw his arms around me.

"Please don't die" my boy cried, hugging me. I never thought about dying I was still feeling invincible at age 39. Perhaps he was right. Maybe I *was* going to die. I had not allowed my mind to go to that place. It was a long night. Joe visited and after he left my ex-husband arrived to let me know he would take me back. After this surgery no one would want me, he said. As my thoughts quickly spanned my 20-year marriage, I laughed out loud. And I needed a laugh! I thought how typical of him and then I realized that sadly, he thought he was being kind. The funny part was that his remarks were not surprising.

After everyone left, the nurses prepared me for the next morning's procedures. Then I was left alone with my thoughts. *What will happen to my son if I die? He is only 18 and we are very close. After all, it had been him and me for the long haul. What about Joe? He is caring, understanding, and makes me laugh. He respects my opinions and pays attention. Will he run away? Certainly, he does not need another problem or responsibility.* That was just the beginning of a very long night.

But somehow in the morning I felt a new sense of resolve. I decided I was going to fight this cancer with everything I had. I knew I had plenty to live for, a circle of good friends, my wonderful son and now a new relationship with a terrific guy.

"Do what you have to do but keep in mind I have just started a new life," I told the doctor.

I need not have worried about Joe deserting me. When he arrived at the hospital he was upbeat and positive. As usual he lit up the room. I was feeling a little bit sorry for myself and within a few short minutes he had me laughing. He was my own personal cheering section.

"Don't you worry, we will get through this together," he said.

"Just tell me what you need." Like everyone else in my network, he was supportive. Like the others he did not leave my side.

When Monday arrived, Nicki and Gerry were at the hospital with me. The time came for my operation and we said our goodbyes. As I was wheeled into the elevator, I looked back and saw tears running down their faces and the fear in their eyes. I just wanted to jump off the stretcher and grab them and tell them it would be all right. Of course, I had no idea it would but I wanted them to feel better. They were such troopers. The next few hours would be even harder on them than on me. I would be asleep.

Later when I opened my eyes and saw Nicki and Gerry standing by my bed, I felt so blessed.

"Was there ever a better sister or friend?" I asked them in a groggy voice.

"No we are the best," Gerry said, smiling.

I immediately put my hand on my left side, felt something and for a fleeting moment I thought, *they made a mistake! I still have my breast!* But then learned that what I felt was just lots and lots of bandage. I had no idea that this would be the first of many operations that I would have over the next 20 years.

The doctor came in to tell me all about the surgery. He said that upon examining the breast tissue, which had been removed, they found three more lesions, also cancerous. There and then they decided to do a mastectomy. I guess this explanation was supposed to make me feel better but how could it? Not only was I in pain, I was also angry and just wanted to be left alone. I knew I was facing a long road, both physically and emotionally. There were tubes in me, drains and IVs hanging out all over me. I was a mess. But mess or not, I had to face day after day poking and prodding and had to submit to physical therapy. Talk about pain! Because muscles had been cut, I would have to learn to use my left arm again.

Upon arriving home from the hospital, I began trying to understand why this happened to me and wondered how I was going to accept my new life. I was assured that my job as manager of operations would be waiting for me. But I was unsure how this trauma would impact my life. I needed to work and was finally in a position to support myself and my son. I knew an experience like this could truly change things for us. I knew I would never again be the person I was before September 13, 1982. I consider myself to be one of those *pull up your boot straps* people, and saw this situation as a tough challenge I would just have to face. But still, I had some nagging thoughts. *Why me I wondered, as so many cancer patients do.* It is natural to want a reason when something bad happens to you. I was convinced I was being punished for divorcing my husband, for tricking him into signing the papers. Perhaps I was being punished for something else I had or had not done. I would need to get past this fruitless kind of thinking.

Nicki took me in and I began my long journey toward recovery. When I wanted to pull the blankets over my head she would not have any of it. She was a tough task-master and a loving and faithful friend. I could not have pulled through without her and the support of her husband and children. I had been protected in a sort of cocoon of safety while recuperating with her. She made sure I ate properly, changed my bandages and told me to stop feeling sorry for myself. Nicki's support and encouragement allowed me to get back home quickly. But back there I had to face what had happened. This was a big step. As I drove into the apartment complex, it started to dawn on me just how hard this was going to be. This was the first time I was alone with my mutilated body. Although my son lived with me, he spent much of his time at his girlfriend Debbie's. But then I had a moment in which I said to myself, *bitter or better?* And that's when I chose to get *better.*

About five weeks after the surgery, the doctor told me that I had healed sufficiently and could think about getting fitted for a prosthesis. I felt less of a woman. My body had been mutilated and, in my eyes, I looked hideous. The thought of anyone seeing me like this was so painful and humiliating it made me sick to my stomach. I was particularly worried about Joe's response. I was convinced his first look at me would send him running. As I stood there looking at myself in the mirror, tears ran down my face I tried to make sense of this moment, however, I was not able to do that until years later. When the day came to be fitted, I realized, once again, as I had as a child, that no one, apart from my nearest and dearest, really had any idea what I was going through. Nor did anyone really care. This was the early '80s, before there were mastectomy boutiques, as they are called today. Back then; these fitting places were frequently in the back of a mom and pop lingerie store. Prostheses were a kind of afterthought to "real" undergarments, a kind of stepchild to the store's saleable merchandise. Fortunately things have changed. Women today who have had mastectomies are treated with far more dignity. Thank goodness!

I went in the store and an old man came out.

"May I help you, Madam?" As my eyes darted around the store. I saw racks of undergarments for women who still had two breasts. I jumped as he spoke and he must have seen a look of terror in my eyes.

"I need to get fitted for prosthesis," I replied in a shaky voice. Wasn't there a woman who could help me? But there seemed to be no one around. He led me into a tiny room and pulled the curtain.

"Just a moment," he said. In a moment, he returned, reached through the curtain and handed me a cotton gown. It was like being back in the hospital.

"Put this on. I will send in my wife when you're undressed." Thank God a woman would be helping me. As I took off my clothes and put on the gown, for the first time I took in my mutilated body in a full-length mirror. My other breast looked lonely next to the flat and scared area where my left breast used to reside. It was so repulsive to me. My hope was that this prosthesis would somehow make it all better.

A short woman with a no-nonsense demeanor came in. She seemed to be in a hurry.

"Got your clothes off, do ya?" She seemed nonchalant, as though I were there to buy a pair of shoes. She gave me orders and with little finesse, measured my remaining breast. The tears on my face did not affect her in the least. She went to a shelf where the breast prostheses were stacked, like shoe boxes. She pulled out several boxes and began to try them on me. They were breast shaped soft and wiggly like a bowl of jello. Filled with silicone, they really did feel real and were weighted to give you balance. Finally she found one that matched my breast. As I tucked the prostheses in my bra I looked in the mirror. Not bad, I thought. This will do.

With this first step done, I was planning on returning to work. I was totally convinced when I walked across the parking lot and through the building that every person would be watching me. That first day I returned, I wore a black skirt and a red scoop neck sweater. I completed the long, seemingly endless walk to my office. Surprisingly, no one was around. The entire staff was upstairs at a meeting. I was delighted because I needed time to adjust after being out of the office for six weeks.

Eventually the staff meeting ended and everyone returned to their work places. Those who had to pass my office simply shouted my way.

"Welcome back!" they said. I was so grateful. Somehow they must have known I don't respond well to sympathy I just wanted everyone to treat me the way they had before. Another big step taken.

I sat in my office acting as if nothing had happened. As if I'd not been gone for two months and was now a woman with one, not two breasts. In the days to come though, I thought about the last two years, and it was clear that so much had happened: so many things in my life had changed. I had gotten divorced, moved, attended my class reunion as a single woman and I had lost my breast. Life could only get better because I couldn't imagine it getting any worse. Then I reflected upon all the *good* things that had happened in the last two years of my life. I was very lucky to have such wonderful friends, especially my not-so-secret angel, Nicki. What would I have done without her?

Along the way there also had been some professional successes. I had worked very hard to advance my career at The Peale Center for Christian Living, where I had begun as a clerk typist. Within a few months I was given the position as the executive secretary to the Executive Editor, Myron L. Boardman. He believed in me and was convinced I was destined for better positions. He was right. I was later promoted to supervisor, then multi-department supervisor, manager and when I retired I was the operations manager with a staff of approximately 50 people reporting to me.

Then there was, most importantly, my relationship with Joe who remained steady and reassuring during the difficult times.

I resolved I would not let my new circumstances get me down. I began volunteering as a counselor with the American Cancer Society in their Reach to Recovery Program. My role was to visit women in the hospital who were about to undergo breast surgery. Of course, they were scared and welcomed a visit from someone who would hold their hand and tell them what to expect. I had not had this and I knew what this kind of support might mean to them. Although I could not guarantee what their futures would hold I thought it would be helpful for them to hear my story, to see someone who was now on the other side of the ordeal. I was a well-dressed professional woman with one breast and I had somehow gone on with my life. I represented encouragement that they could one day look like themselves again.

I also started a support group for single and divorced women. We gathered at my home once a week for a casual meeting with light snacks and lots of real talk about relationships. Some of the stories were horrors and some women wanted opportunities to vent, but there is no question that the camaraderie and sisterhood helped all involved. These activities created a positive influence in my life and in the lives of the people I met. Some of the women were absolutely wonderful, others truly an inspiration. In truth, they helped me as much as I helped them. Things were looking up and it was at this time that I decided to go for reconstructive surgery. Surgery number two.

Even though I encouraged the women I visited before and after their mastectomies they would be alright, in truth, the loss of my breast was very difficult for me. It was, in fact, so difficult that I was unable to accept it as a loss. A year after my original surgery I made the difficult decision to embark on yet another adventure. At least this one was of my choosing. I researched the possibilities of reconstructive surgery, eliminating implants, since they were a foreign substance which my body might reject. In my research I discovered a procedure that would use my own body muscle and tissue to build a breast. This procedure seemed both interesting and exciting, although I was a bit daunted when I learned that the operation could take more than seven hours. I let some time go by before I made my final decision.

I met with the doctor who developed this unique procedure. He was from Israel and his work involved training American doctors to perform this operation. I was delighted when he told me I was a perfect candidate. For this operation the large stomach muscle is removed, brought up through the body, and placed in the chest cavity. The muscle, along with a little body fat, creates a new breast. He explained that doctors would only perform this surgery on patients who were in excellent physical condition and had very strong stomach muscles, because one of your stomach muscles would be sacrificed. I was a bit of an exercise fanatic and was very proud of the fact that I did 500 sit-ups every day. Because of that I had a stomach like a rock. I was delighted that I "qualified," and we began to make arrangements for me to have the surgery.

It took six weeks to make all the plans and the entire time I experienced a combination of excitement and tremendous fear. The weekend before the big day I was very busy getting things ready and packing for the hospital and the two-week recovery period. Then a disappointing phone call came in.

"The surgery has been cancelled," a nurse told me.

"What?!"

"The doctors could not organize a way to get paid," she explained. I could not believe that professionals could make these decisions that would impact the lives of their patients. What happened to all the supportive words I had heard from the famous surgeon from Israel? For me this type of behavior was all too familiar. I had to remind myself that I didn't matter!

"The doctor who would be performing the surgery is going back to Israel and a local doctor would be taking charge of the aftercare," the nurse explained. How the payment for the aftercare would be divided became a problem.

"This presents a conflict, so we have had to cancel."

I was angry, really angry. The doctors could not agree on the details, so they cancelled everything? Money. It was all about the money! I felt so empty, knowing the doctors made decision based on money with no real regard for human feelings or emotional life. I wanted to go to the top of a mountain and scream! Old feelings came back to haunt me, feelings related to how my life had been decided by others and not by me.

I thought of giving up on the idea and then I would change my mind. *Why should I let these greedy doctors spoil my plans?* I did a lot of soul searching. *Yes, no, yes, no.* Then finally I came to the place where I knew I would not quit. I would do more research to find another doctor trained to perform this surgery.

In a matter of days I was lucky enough to find a doctor who had offices in nearby Westchester and New York City. After weeks of discussion and exams, I was scheduled for surgery again. On that critical day, my sister and Nicki drove me to the hospital. The ride was quiet without much conversation.

"So tell me what you are thinking?" Nicki asked.

"Quite frankly, I'm thinking that maybe we should turn this car around and go home."

"Oh, is that really what you want me to do?" She looked over at me.

"No, keep driving" I said. As I was being admitted, my emotions surged up. I kept thinking of my last experience and got scared and apprehensive but I would not turn back.

The surgery was scheduled for 7:30 a.m. More than twelve hours later, I awoke in my room, feeling as if I had been run over by a really big truck. In my entire life, I had never experienced such pain. It felt like someone was constantly stabbing me in the stomach with a very dull knife. Gerry and Nicki, supportive as they were, couldn't really do or say anything to make it better. Their presence was a comfort though, and I was lucky to have someone there to summon the nurses for pain medication, since I simply did not have the strength myself. It was a long night, but I was kept pretty drugged and so I slept.

In the morning the nurses wanted me to get out of bed. *Impossible*, I thought. Who are you kidding! It would be three days before I was able to get up and move. When I did finally get out of bed, I was convinced I would never walk upright again. I was bent over like a very old woman and in agony. But the doctors and nurses said it was imperative that I walk around. This is part of the healing process. And I was determined to heal.

Seven

How could I know this would be nothing compared to what was to come? There would be more physical distress and emotional turmoil. As the days went by after that reconstructive surgery, I faced a very rough time. The morning after the surgery I laid there in disbelief. I had tubes coming out of every place possible and I was so heavily bandaged I could not move. The pain was so intense I didn't think I could bare it. The highlight of my day was when the nurse arrived with pain medication and that would be the case for several days. When I was alone and allowed myself to think about what had happened the last few years, my heart ached and my spirit felt so wounded. But then I pushed those thoughts away. Somehow I had convinced myself this surgery would make me whole again. I could get dressed and not worry about making sure my breast was positioned properly. Physically that was true but psychologically I knew I had a lot of work to do. I still questioned my decision to have this reconstructive surgery and I wanted the results to be perfect. I had to be practical. I had learned through my life that there is no such thing as perfect. I just wanted to look and feel normal.

When it was time to have the dressings changed, I had a look at my new breast. The doctor arrived bright and early and I was very excited. As I sat on the edge of the bed he began of remove the bandages the process seemed to go on forever.

"So doc what do you think. Am I centerfold material?" He laughed.

"Oh Joanne, I think you are going to love this result." He seemed very proud of his work and all smiles.

"This looks like a perfect match to your natural breast."

"Okay doc, it's my turn. Can you get me a mirror?" When he returned with the mirror I was so excited however, it took me a couple of minutes to hold it and take my first look. The size and shape looked about right, but I was concerned because it was very bruised. The doctor said that was to be expected and assured me that it was normal. I was pleased and apprehensive at the same time.

After a few days I was discharged but since I could not be alone yet, Nicki took me home with her yet again. I know I could not have survived this ordeal without her. She was my strength, my courage, and most of all, the best friend anyone could hope to have. We both had no idea what was ahead I could never have realized that I was entering one of the most emotionally and physically difficult periods of my life.

Every day Nicki changed my bandages; cooked for me and made sure I got up and walked around. I would probably still be walking bent over if Nicki had not been there to support me every step of the way and coax me into doing the right thing. She was a tough taskmaster. She would come into my room every hour or so and insist I get up, walk around and stand up straight. The incision to remove my stomach muscle had caused me to walk bent and I was convinced I would never stand totally upright again.

"Come on now, stop being a baby and walk into the kitchen. We can play a game of cards." Though I was not interested in cards or much else all it would take was one stern look from her before I got up and did what she asked. I slept in the guest bedroom which, at the time, seemed about a mile from the kitchen where she would proceed to beat me at cards. We spent hours talking and she continually assured me I would one day walk upright! But as time went by, I became increasingly concerned about the healing of my breast. I continued to go to the doctor and he continued to encourage me, saying that everything would be all right.

It was not all right! My new breast was dying. The tissue smelled like a rotting rodent that had died behind the wall, a sure sign that all was *not* well. The ironic thing is that I felt physically better each day and was almost walking upright. Joe would pick me up and bring me to his house for one of his mother's wonderful dinners. He was very supportive and concerned when I would tell him about what was going on with my new breast. During this period we spoke everyday but did not see too much of each other. His work, children and mother took much of his time and I was consumed with my healing process. Each week I went to the doctor and he would remove the dead tissue from my new breast and send me home. The process was dreadful as well as gruesome. As I lay on the table, tears running down my face, he stood, scalpel in his hand.

"Relax," he would say. Oh yeah, like that's going to happen with a doctor taking a scalpel to your breast and cutting away the tissue that had died. I don't think so. The procedure is called debreeding, the cutting away of dead tissue. He had not yet determined why the tissue was dying. I would later learn that the stomach muscle used to build my new breast had needed a blood supply. The doctor had taken an artery from my groin and attached it to the stomach muscle. This should have been the blood supply for my new breast, however, scar tissue had formed around the artery and cut off the blood supply and now the new breast was dying.

"I am sure something is not right," I would say, but he assured me I was doing fine.

Then, a couple of months later, I insisted. To continue hoping he could cut away enough dead skin and hopefully save this breast was masochistic on my part. I demanded answers.

"Joanne, it's time to end this I had hoped it would work but I can see it will not." I just stared at him, tears welling up in my eyes.

"You knew this would happen, didn't you? I can't believe you allowed this to go on so long," I screamed at him. He did not respond.

"Wasn't this a new procedure and still considered experimental?" He agreed it was. I had been right all along.

And so on January 5th, my 41st birthday, I entered the hospital to have this new breast removed. Instead of getting a gift for my birthday, I was having one taken away. It was a dark period of my life, which my mind has protected me from remembering, flushing out many of the details. I do remember that I was so angry with the doctor, who had kept encouraging me to hang in there, assuring me that everything would be okay. He obviously did not want to admit the surgery had failed. I hated him, mentally putting him in the same category as those greedy doctors. You remember them the ones who couldn't figure out how to pay for aftercare when the surgeon returned to Israel. But my hateful feelings and anger and rage towards these doctors were not helping me to heal. In addition, I was feeling I was somehow not deserving of a successful result. I was feeding on all those malingering, ever-haunting feelings of unworthiness and shame I felt as a child. Would they ever go away?

The only bright light during this process was my growing relationship with Joe. He was a faithful and devoted partner. What Joe had to deal with when we were together was the stench of a dying body part. However, he said he never was aware of the odor. I remember the odor so clearly that it would be many months before I would not smell it even long after the removal of the breast.

Somehow Joe never seemed to care he was always so incredibly supportive. This debacle began within the first two years of our relationship and fortunately for me he was a leg man! He told me many times that he did not fall in love with my breasts; he fell in love with me. During this difficult time I replayed those words over and over in my head. Once in a while I wondered if he were the kind of man who would stick around only until I was well. Then he would bolt. But in my heart of hearts, the man I was hopelessly in love with would not do that.

My surgery for the removal of the new breast was scheduled for early the next morning. It had been less than 24 hours since the doctor admitted that my breast was dying and I would have to endure another surgical procedure. I woke up and there was Joe gazing down at me. All of a sudden I was filled with hope. He always did that for me. He is one of the most positive people I have ever met. After a good morning kiss and his usual words of encouragement, I was on my way to the operating room. It took a lot less time to remove this breast than it did to create it. Barely awake from the surgery, I was told that I needed skin graft to close the gaping hole in my chest. The removal of the dead breast had destroyed any viable skin. *Skin graft,* I thought. *More surgery. I can't, I just can't do this.* But I had to. What I did now know was that skin graft was a simple procedure of laying harvested skin on the affected area and waiting for it to take.

The skin graft was done over a period of several days. As I lay there my thoughts wandered back to my childhood. I thought of how my siblings and I overcame so many difficult times. The fire, the foster homes, and the fact that we had no one to love us. But we did have each other and I resolved that what I was facing would not be so difficult after all. I had been through a lot worse.

A few days passed and I went home to recover and mourn the loss of yet another breast. And mourn I did. It wasn't just the loss of my new breast but the seeming continual series of things going wrong in my quest to make them right. Would I ever feel normal again? I was feeling sorry for myself and found comfort wallowing in my own self-pity. I'd been so close to achieving a sense of normalcy in my physical and emotional life and then had had this setback. Yes, I had Joe in my life. I had my son, but this series of setbacks triggered old self-esteem issues. I felt so defeated and unworthy, could this situation be corrected? Now I wondered if I would ever get my life on track. I just wanted to be able to get dressed and not have to stuff a sock in my bra. Why was that so difficult? Maybe successful results were reserved for the "good" people, and not for those like me. I had lived my life always believing I was less than worthy and there was always someone or something to reinforce those feelings. First my mother's rejection, then foster care placements, my failed marriage and now this. I didn't get it, I was that person who always tried to do the right thing but somehow it was never enough. So why did I think this would work?

I spent the next couple of weeks getting used to the skin graft and its healing. Finally something went right and the graft was taking. There I was lying in bed with my mutilated breast and the doctor was laying pieces of skin on the area. That's all it was. You just lay the skin on the area and hope that it takes. I was trying to put this hideous experience behind me when my surgeon suggested he could make things even better. Again and again he asked me to let him try an implant because he was convinced this would work. An implant would make me look normal he said. I believe he felt so bad that the surgery was a failure and wanted to compensate me for that. I told him that I would give it a lot of thought. I had been through an awful lot of surgery and was not sure I wanted to go through anymore. It was hard enough just trying to get through a day without crying, being angry and simply learning to look at myself.

After the removal of the new breast and the ensuing skin graft, my chest looked as though someone had taken a hatchet to it. The attempt to correct it had only made it worse. There was not a sufficient amount of skin to cover the crevices in my chest. The caliber of this work was so poor it looked and felt as though it was an afterthought, not a well thought-out, caring process.

Because it was getting more and more difficult for me to look at myself, I agreed to yet another surgery the following year. There were people who thought that I was crazy, or that perhaps I had become addicted to the idea of surgery. It might have looked that way, but this was not the case. Of course, I would have preferred to be done with the whole thing. But in the end I did decide to go for another reconstructive surgery. I was going to finish what I had started; finally, I felt I deserved something better. I allowed myself some time to heal both physically and psychologically, before I made a decision.

So here I was facing surgery number six. Perhaps taking this risk was a little crazy, but I had come so far already, so why not? This surgery would involve a two-step process. First, the surgeon would place a tissue expander in my chest, which he would then fill with saline solution every two weeks. Once that was done, the expanded skin would be able to accept an implant. Just the expanding process alone took a few weeks, so this required patience and faith.

Then came the next piece, surgeries seven and eight. The skin graft would not expand sufficiently to match the right breast. I had to agree to have the surgeon operate on my right breast, reducing it in size to match the implant that would go on the left. I was getting in deeper and deeper and the whole process was becoming more and more convoluted but I kept going. As I thought about going forward I continued questioning my decision to proceed. Joe was his usual supportive self. He assured me that whatever decision I would make he would support. He also continued to reassure me he was a leg man! Our relationship never skipped a beat and the surgeries did not impact our intimate life.

As I checked in for this surgery I was uneasy and very scared. The room somehow seemed much smaller the walls felt as if they were closing in on me. I got into the bed and the nurses began the usual pre-op preparation.

"Back again?" my nurse said sarcastically.

"Yes, I am really nervous about tomorrow's procedure."

"Well just remember this is called elective surgery you can change your mind." The nurse took my blood pressure and the cuff seemed tighter than usual and the thermometer seemed to have a funny taste. They had painted the rooms and changed the curtains since my last stay. The nurses seemed very busy and unusually quiet. I felt like I was in their way.

"Do you need anything? We are very busy with really sick patients so I will probably not be back here before my shift is over."

"Oh no I am fine." I did not understand her attitude. I felt dismissed by her. The hustle and bustle was loud and fast and as I sat on the edge of the bed the room began to spin. I tried to stand up and decided against that. I laid back and watched the room slowly spin and the nurse never came back that night. However the doctor came in and asked how I was doing. He was a short man with light graying hair. He asked me to follow him to an examining room. He needed to draw lines on my breasts, which would guide the placement of the left implant and removal of tissue to reduce my right breast. I stood against the wall while he used a marker to draw lines on my right breast. I stood there, drenched with perspiration, wearing nothing more than a pair of bikini panties while a man marked up my body. I felt so humiliated. Although I had elected this surgery, the process was horrific, every last bit of it.

The night before the surgery, Joe came to visit. In an effort to help me relax, he brought along a tape player and a tape of music by Brian Eno, called *Music for Airports*. I was in some mood, apprehensive and second-guessing my decision, thinking about cancelling everything. Joe, however, listened patiently to my ranting.

"Can you believe the attitude of that nurse?" I fluffed the pillow behind me and pulled and tugged on the bedding.

"I can't believe she would say that to me. She acted like I was taking up a bed from a really sick person."

Joe looked over his glasses as he was attentively listening and setting up the tape player at the same time.

"Well let me tell you….." My hands went to my face and I began to cry. Joe wrapped his arms around me.

"Don't worry about her. She's probably just having a bad day." I wiped my eyes.

"Well she made me feel guilty for choosing to have this surgery."

"She can only do that if you allow her to." As we talked Joe finished setting up the tape player and before long the room began to fill with the relaxing sounds of Brian Eno's music. I fell off to sleep, never heard Joe leave and when I awoke I was ready to face the ordeal as planned. On my way to the operating room, I understood the surgeon was very pleased to have the chance to correct the failed previous surgery. With the bright lights blinding me, the clanking of surgical instruments as the surgical crew discussed their lives; my nurse smiled and leaned into me.

"The procedure did not fail. It was your body that failed to accept the tissue," she assured me. I needed to set her straight.

"No," I shook my head.

"The tissue died. My body did not reject it and I just hope this time it is successful." The next thing I knew the surgery was over and I was in the recovery room.

This time it was a longer procedure because of the additional work to reduce the right breast. When I awoke in the recovery room, I was groggy and in so much pain. Once again I was confronted with the blasé and uncaring attitude of the nursing staff. With their behavior, they seem to suggest that because you have chosen to have the surgery then you need to be prepared for the pain. No complaining! Not only do they seem unaware of the physical pain, but also they certainly have *no clue* as to the *emotional* pain. The nurses seemed unaware that I was having this surgery as a result of cancer and a mastectomy. This procedure was very new and the previous surgery was cutting-edge. Even as I write this section I am still amazed at the treatment I received from the hospital staff. What happened to women supporting women? I believed then and still do today that some females are women's worst enemies.

That evening I met my two roommates, a young girl and an older woman. We were a rather incompatible trio. The young girl was recuperating from surgery for a brain tumor and the older woman, a doctor's wife, had had a hysterectomy. I believe that this older woman was quite upset that she was being made to share a room with two cancer patients, as she complained continuously about the young woman's moaning.

But my heart was with this young girl who was so agitated after her surgery. She was whining, crying, and so were her family members the whole group was in a terrible state. Joe being Joe suggested to the husband that perhaps the tape player and tape which had helped to calm me would help calm his young wife. The man accepted. "I will try anything to ease her pain," he said. They played music for the rest of the evening, much to the chagrin of the doctor's wife. This young girl had a peaceful, restful night, despite all her discomfort. The next morning the nurse asked for a copy of the tape and vowed to play it for all post-operative patients.

As I prepared to go home, a nurse approached me.

"Well are you finished with all this surgery stuff or what?"

I was shocked, speechless. She obviously had not had training in patient relations. But to be fair, there had been other nurses who exhibited great compassion. I remember one nurse in particular. When I woke in the recovery room I was freezing cold and shaking. All of a sudden she was covering me with a heated blanket and at that moment I loved her.

Upon my arrival home and back into my everyday life, I still had to confront other people who displayed an attitude similar to that of the nurses. There seemed to be an endless number of people who wouldn't hesitate to voice their opinions about decisions that affected my physical and mental health. I encountered a sheer lack of understanding and empathy from many individuals from whom I expected more. I suppose it is hard for people to comment with understanding and compassion on issues they just do not understand.

The surgery left me less than satisfied. I had sacrificed a portion of my good breast and it did not come close to matching the implant. I was now clearly asymmetrical. What I did not know at that point was that the implant had immediately encapsulated, which means it simply hardens to the point where it looks and feels nothing like a real breast. Apart from looking terrible, it also causes pain and constant discomfort. This was the result of a poorly carried out operation. I would later learn that the initial process of placing the expander was not left in my chest long enough. The doctor only waited a few weeks before he removed it and replaced it with an implant. The expander should have been left in for a few months.

As time passed I accepted that this was as good as it was going to get. I would just have to learn to live with the result. But after about a year, I began to notice sores in my mouth and an aching in my joints. I feared that what I had read in articles and heard in the news was true for me this could be the direct result of the silicone implant. After much research and discussions with Joe, I decided to have the silicone implant removed and replaced with a saline implant. Because I had had so many surgeries I thought maybe I should not do this, but fear and health concerns generated my decision.

My plastic surgeon tentatively agreed to go ahead with this procedure. I had developed sores in my mouth and was experiencing pains in my joints, which studies had shown were directly connected to implants.

But he seemed to hesitate about setting a date.

"You know, Joanne, all this surgery is getting out of hand" he finally said. At this point, I began to second-guess myself and every decision I would make. As I sat in the surgeon's office I made up my mind this would be the last surgery he would perform on me. I was done! As I checked in for this procedure I was pleased to find out it was one-day surgery. They wheeled me into the operating room and my head was spinning. There were lines of stretchers in the hall waiting for their turn. I was immediately transported back to my early days at the children's home with the metal beds lined up along the wall. I needed to shake off those thoughts and as the doctor administered the anesthesia my thoughts shifted to the best thing in my life Joe. When I awoke I felt safer about my health but I did not feel good about my appearance. My right breast was larger than the implant. The implant was misshapen and lower than my right breast. Again, I had to accept that this was as good as it was going to get. I wanted to move forward with my life and think about something else, something more joyful and light. The aching and sores did not completely heal, but I learned to live with them. I really wanted to stop fighting with my own body.

Eight

After five years of dating, I moved in with Joe. It was a very big step for both of us. I had mixed feelings about leaving my condo, since I had worked so hard to get to this place of independence and self-sufficiency. I had regained my financial stability, which had been all but obliterated during the divorce. When I was able to qualify for a mortgage and buy my apartment it represented a major victory for me. I just could not let go of the place and decided to rent it out. In the back of my mind I also considered if things did not go well for us, I would have the safety net I needed.

But it did work out. We lived together for two years then married. During our two-year life before our wedding I set out to cement my relationship with Joe's children, John and Kerry. It was made easier for me because I was there for Joe and the kids however, I did not have to deal with the discipline. Joe took that responsibility. Kerry joined me on shopping trips, work-outs at the gym and many lunches and before you knew it we were great friends. Remember they were teenagers and had a mom. I represented the female voice in the house. It was such a joy to come home from work, prepare a meal and have everyone at the table appreciative. After two years of living together and feeling in our heart of hearts that this would work, we decided to marry.

It was a simple wedding in a tent in our backyard. We made the choice to get married at home because Joe's mother, Ann, who was very ill, would not have been able to attend if she had had to travel. Despite our plans for her convenience and comfort, though, Ann passed away six weeks before our wedding. Her passing was a huge blow to our little family. She was an incredible human being and I was so angry that I would never get to call her Mom! I loved her and I miss her. I often think back to our girl-talk sessions. Such fun!

Now we were very conflicted about what to do. We did not feel comfortable sending out wedding invitations with so much grief among family members. At Ann's funeral, though, Joe's Aunt Tess, the family matriarch, approached us.

"Send out the invitations and proceed with the wedding! After all, that is what my sister would have wanted," she said. With that blessing, we went ahead with our plans.

And so on October 8, 1988, our backyard was beautifully adorned with flowers, a big white tent, and a graceful arch, draped with flowers and greens. It was a setting fit for a queen and I did feel like a queen that day. I was determined this time to include those special touches that made the day perfect. The only problem was it was snowing when I got up and then the snow turned to rain. I had always been told that that was good luck and hoped it was true. I flashed back to my first wedding day. Everett's mother had pretty much planned the whole wedding. It was in the church and there was cake and finger foods served. As my brother Ron walked me down the aisle I was ashamed I did not have the courage to turn and run. My wedding to Joe, what a great day. Even the snow that turned to rain was welcome. Happily, when the ceremony was over the sun came out and a rainbow appeared. I planned every little detail and moment and it was a day filled with pure joy. However, I can't take credit for the rainbow!

It was a very special family event. Joe's son John, was the best man, his daughter Kerry my maid of honor. My son, Everett, gave me away. My former boss, Colonel Porter, a retired army chaplain, preformed the ceremony. As Everett walked me from the house to the wedding tent down a path draped with beautiful flowers, he held and umbrella over us to hold off the rain. As I entered the tent my first glimpse was of Joe standing there, his hands crossed in front of him. My heart skipped a beat! He was dressed in a light gray tuxedo with a dusty rose cumber bun and I wore a mid-calf ivory lace dress over a dusty rose camisole. We all felt Ann's presence and spirit as we looked around and saw our family and friends and we felt their joy for us. When we were presented to our guests as Mr. and Mrs. Joseph Bellontine the tent exploded with cheers and applause. There was barely a dry eye among the guests. As our guests congratulated us we were overwhelmed by their happiness for us. Knowing we had such support from friends and family made all the difference and gave us a great start to our life together. In an effort to lessen the stress of life and maximize the pleasure on my wedding day, I did not tell my mother I was getting married. I simply did not want her there, creating emotional conflict for me. I truly felt she was never there for me in the tough times and I certainly did not need her now.

A week after the wedding I called her and told her to address my mail to *Joanne Bellontine.* I knew that what I had done might be considered by some to be small, petty, or even hateful, but deep inside I felt satisfied with my decision. To be somewhat kind, though, and spare my mother's feelings, I told her that I had not "burdened" her with an invitation because her husband Paul, of nine years was sick. That was a lie. I also said that I did not want to cause additional stress by putting her in a position in which she would have to leave Paul to attend my wedding, another lie. I don't know whether or not she believed me, but the deed was done now, so it was a moot point. I was married. I am ashamed to admit I really didn't care. She had spent her life just caring about herself and wanting to be center stage, I was not giving her an opportunity to parade around as the Mother of the Bride or be part of the happiest day of my life! A day she had nothing to do with. In a monotone voice, my mother congratulated me and said she hoped I would finally have the happiness I deserved. She did think Joe was great and as the years passed mom and Joe would have many early morning conversations when she came to visit. Those conversations, passed between the two of them allowed me to learn many details about my mother's life.

This time around marriage was a good thing. Sometimes I would wake before Joe and, just lay there and watch him sleep. Life was good and I had no regrets. We knew we were blessed in so many ways; our children all got along and seemed to really like each other. This was the harmonious blending of two families, which was so important for me. I had come from a discordant family background, confused and broken apart, and now I could have something whole even better than whole, in fact. I was grateful to have come this far.

Nine

For the next few years, I concentrated on my marriage, family and work. Everything was moving along smoothly and successfully. The children were growing and thriving. John had graduated from high school and entered college and Kerry would soon be on her way to college. Everett had married the year before Joe and I did, and two years later presented us with a beautiful granddaughter, Lauren, born August 15, 1989. She would be our only grandchild for the next ten years. Grandchildren change your life, if you choose to be involved in raising them. We chose to be very involved, having Lauren stay with us frequently on weekends. Of course, we were always eager to babysit. Kerry was still living at home and loved spending time with her new niece. As Lauren grew, Kerry would spend hours doing crafts with her and teaching her how to match her socks to her shirt. Life was good!

Our home became the hub of family activity. Lauren once described it so well in a picture she drew, where our house was in the middle. It seemed out of place with the rest of the picture; I asked her why she had put our house in the middle

"It's the gathering place, Grandma," she said. I love that description. All holidays and family events would take place at our home, and we are only too happy about that. Because as a child I had no permanent home, no sense of family, warmth, or security, this is paramount. My children, grandchildren, and the whole family unit are my most precious gifts.

In the summer of 2002, I was at an appointment with my oncologist and as he examined me he suggested that I see an up-and-coming plastic surgeon.

"I know that he can fix that mess on your chest," he told me. I looked at him as though he had lost his mind. More surgery? Yikes! What could possess anyone to think I would volunteer for that? But this doctor was not aware of all that I had been through to create this *mess*, as he called it. Oh boy was it a mess. My left breast looked like a piece of chopped meat, way smaller than my right breast, bumpy, discolored, and extremely misshapen. It was covered with scars and had a misplaced nipple. What a sight. What a travesty. I had learned to live with this breast but I never came to terms with it. I have to say that it never bothered Joe; our intimate life never skipped a beat. However, emotionally every time I would undress and get into bed with Joe I felt I was less of a woman and that he deserved more. My stuff, I know! However, the thought of additional surgery seemed way too scary. Why should I think that some up-and-coming plastic surgeon could fix this mess?

"I will think about it," I told him, but I was just humoring him. I wanted to get out of that office as quick as possible.

That night a dinner I told Joe about my doctor visit.

"Can you imagine," I said.

"He suggested I see another plastic surgeon! Does he think I am crazy? Or is he crazy?"

"Why not?" Joe asked. We were eating dinner and he was slicing open a roll. He held the knife in his hand.

"There is no harm in finding out what he might be able to do," he said.

"After all, a lot has changed in the surgical field and who knows he may be able to fix it." I watched him butter his roll. He knew how *my mess* upset me. This was very much Joe's style; he always gave me full support. The next day, I went on the Internet and looked up this new plastic surgeon, Dr. Douglas Roth. His credentials were impressive, as was the wide spectrum of *individualized and dignified patient care,* which had been sorely lacking in all the doctors I had seen so far. Part of me still felt I had really lost all sense of reason, but I called and made an appointment. Little did I know how important this man would become in my life.

When I arrived at the office, I started to think more optimistically, less skeptically. Maybe he could fix this mess that was my body. After all the surgeries I never gave up hope that one day I could look close to normal. Surgery after surgery and this thing I called my breast just kept getting worse. Wouldn't that be great? But then I was taken out of my daydreaming and asked to come in for the exam. Dr. Roth, a soft-spoken man with the most extraordinary manner, was probably the first doctor in this whole process that really seemed to care. He was young and so personable, married with two beautiful little daughters whom he said he took on rounds on weekends. He truly seemed to feel my pain and wanted to make it better.

Before the exam he asked all about me and what I had experienced through the reconstruction process. I told him the whole terrible story. Then we proceeded to the actual exam. As he looked at my body, Dr. Roth noticed a bulge in my abdomen.

"What is this?" he asked.

"It looks like a hernia."

"Oh that?" I said.

"I have had that for at least eighteen years. It was a result of my first botched attempt at breast reconstruction."

He was shocked.

"Mrs. Bellontine, whether or not you decide to have the reconstructive surgery, *this* has to be fixed. I know a surgeon who can take care of that for you."

I took his direction and made an appointment with the surgeon. Upon seeing me, it did not take him long to ascertain the problem.

"Yes, this bulge is an abdominal hernia."

"Why is it dangerous?" I asked.

"It could rupture at any time, and if it does, you will find yourself with your intestines sitting in your lap, or worse! It must be fixed immediately."

Despite his warning, though, I didn't get too alarmed. I had lived with this condition for 18 years. But I did consider it another mess in my life that reminded me of all I'd been through. My journey through the world of surgery was truly an exercise in trying to heal myself from the outside in. I was working hard to make sense out of this travesty which had now gone on for so many years. I thought I can only finish getting better if I fix my physical appearance. I thought back to when I first saw this bulge and had asked my original surgeon about it.

"Don't worry about it," he assured me.

"It's no big deal." I suppose I should have been more aggressive, more of an advocate for myself. Curiously, with all the doctors I have seen, not one ever asked about it. I would be lying down during the exam, making the bulge less noticeable. In retrospect, though, I should have brought it to their attention. But I didn't. I had been through so much, and I probably didn't want to make more waves in my life.

So now I had two problems, both equally urgent and both plaguing me. I wanted to eradicate them and found a way to address both of my problems at the same time. When I visited the surgeon for the hernia, I explained I was also trying to have my breast reconstructed. Amazingly, he agreed to work with Dr. Roth, thus making it possible to fix the two conditions at the same time. This plan would require a *third* surgery involving a tissue expander and an insertion of a new implant, and the process would take a full five months. I decided to go for it. Although I had been through so much surgery already, and this would surely be quite invasive, I was willing to go through with it. I wanted to finish this once and for all, to finally see my life in balance. I could not imagine too many of my friends and family members making such a choice for their physical and emotional healing, but I knew I just had to move forward.

Joe, more than anyone else, knew what correcting these medical conditions would mean to me, and he was with me all the way. We woke early; I showered while Joe had his coffee. As I dressed I gazed into the half steamed mirror and silently said good bye to my hideous breast. As I came down the stairs Joe had backed the car down the lawn and left it running to warm up. Joe had come back into the house and was waiting for me.

"Need a ride lady?" We smiled and were on our way to the hospital at 6 a.m. for my surgery. As with all the times before, the nursing staff prepped me and we rolled down the hall. My wonderful and supportive husband waited patiently to hear that the operation was completed.

After a couple of hours, the surgeon looked for Joe in the waiting area. He had a question for him.

"I thought your wife said she had a saline implant," he said.

"What I found in there was silicone. Can you shed some light on this?" Joe didn't know how to respond.

"Additionally," the doctor continued.

"Silicone was scattered all over the breast cavity."

Joe was stunned. He thought back on the pain I had suffered in 1989, when I had specifically elected the saline implant because of the sores in my mouth and aches in my joints.

When I awoke, Joe had to tell me what he had learned from the doctor. This put my mind into a tailspin, wondering if that doctor had even removed the original implant! Obviously he had not. Apparently he just cut me open and closed me up again with a few new stitches to appease me. The sense of having been violated in this way was beyond description, and only over time has the dismay subsided. In fact, *too* much time had gone by for us to pursue a case of malpractice. If I let my mind go to that place, I remember the mutilation of the body and the disregard for me as a human being. It is better not to dwell on it and instead, focus on how I have repaired this condition.

It was a long spring and summer. My new plastic surgeon expanded my skin to the right size, and then left the expander in for some additional time to be sure the skin would not shrink back. Every few weeks I would go to Dr. Roth's office and he would inflate the expander with saline solution. It took five months to get to the stage where I was ready to exchange the expander for the silicone implant, which, by the way, is reserved only for those patients who have had breast cancer. (Research has not yet determined whether silicone implants can be used simply for elective breast augmentation.) As the time grew closer, again my mind was filled with doubt. Was I doing the right thing? Would this work this time or would it be just another step in the debacle of my breast? I would close my eyes to sleep and all I could see was my mutilated breast. Oh please let it be okay this time!

On Friday, September 13, 2002, fortunately I was not superstitious and the date did not scare me, as a matter of fact, I thought it was a lucky omen. It had been exactly twenty years to the day from my original mastectomy. I was now scheduled for what I hoped would be the final surgery on this breast. Oh my poor breast had been through a debacle, like a piece of land that has been invaded, trampled over, and cut up. At 4:30 a.m. I was lying awake, my mind going a thousand miles an hour with emotions, excitement, terror, but greatest of all, hope. Dr. Roth had promised me a result that would satisfy, and while I wanted that to be true, I was well aware that I had been promised these results before and was bitterly disappointed. The experts tell you it will be all right and you want to believe them. What other choice do you have? I have learned the hard way that this is frequently not true, and so my mind continued to circle in the early morning hours, until daylight came.

Once again, Joe and I drove to the surgery center, this time with little talk. He tried to distract me, but I couldn't converse. I had my own whirlwind of questions going through my head. *When I get there will I go through with it?* I wondered. *Would this operation be a success or would I have to go through more of what I had just experienced?* The questions raced around in my head like a rocket ship.

Upon arrival, we checked in and this time I found the folks very kind and understanding. That was just what I needed, and their kindness brought me to tears. Like all humans, sometimes I am vulnerable, like a small child who needs to know that someone bigger, stronger, and smarter will take charge and do the right thing.

Now on the operating table, I saw the first person to arrive the anesthesiologist, who offered me a feel-good cocktail. As I submitted once again to the hospital procedures and drifted slowly into a dream state, I thought of my husband and beautiful grandchildren and saw them as the reason I had to live, to be well. I had so many more years of life that I wanted to enjoy with them with Joe, with my children, and our family. So much to live for, and I was determined to live and feel well for all of it. Strangely, despite the number of surgeries I had had, I still was not use to giving up control. I was still not free from fear. My mind went round and round with thoughts like, *have I been given the right amount of anesthesia? Will I wake up again?*

9:30 a.m. I was wheeled out into the recovery area. Someone who sensed that I was cold placed a pre-warmed blanket over me. It felt wonderful, cocoon-like, and safe. I wanted to stay and sleep. But soon, I was being awakened, and then suddenly, I couldn't wait to go home. The ride back to our house was gentle and quiet. I didn't feel like talking; all I could think of was getting into bed, deep in the safety of our home. I spent the rest of the day in solitude, just needing to rest.

The next day I felt that I had awakened into a new life. This was the day I had been waiting for, for 20 years, one in which all of these problems would be over for good. I awoke to find the sun shining into our room, and its brilliance forced me to open my eyes. My first thought was that I had survived the previous day's events. There was some pain and a feeling of the stitches "pulling," but I had known that pain before.

Just as I needed attention, Joe appeared in the doorway with coffee, water and pain medication. That's Joe focused, attentive and compassionate. Sometimes I think Joe makes up for all the deficiencies of the people of my life. His love has, in a sense, affected the misery of the past the unfeeling people, the incapable parents, the insensitive educators, and incompetent medical professionals. He has redeemed them all. And in this particularly fragile state, I was aware of this more than ever.

This day could only move slowly. I was reluctant to remove my garments and bandages to view the surgeon's artistry and decided to put it off until later. I needed to eat and rest some more, and in the late afternoon, I gathered up the courage to take a look. Hobbling into the bathroom, I knew I would have to remove those dreaded bandages.

Slowly, slowly, I took off my nightshirt and began the delicate and arduous process. It was only a small bandage, but in my state of mind it seemed like rolls and rolls of gauze. I took a deep breath, wanting so much for everything to be all right this time. What I saw was exciting and very scary, an almost perfect left breast.

As the days past, the swelling began to subside and the breast began to take on a life of its own. I made several visits to Dr. Roth; stitches were removed and my new breast began to take on its own personality. Before, I'd look at it and just see a lump of flesh. Now there was a real breast there, a breast that demanded attention, saying,

"Hey, Joanne! I'm not just a blob, I'm a real breast and need something pretty to wear!" A few days after the swelling went down, I had the courage to dig deep into my dresser and pull out that Victoria's Secret bra. It was a beauty, hot pink and black! How I had been waiting to try it on! And so I did, and for the first time in two decades, I not only *felt* like a whole woman, I *looked* like one. I wondered where Dr. Roth was back when this whole episode started. Then I realized he was probably still in grade school. I finally met a doctor who knew what he was talking about and knew what he was doing. He had not only promised to make it better, he did. I hold him in the highest regard in the medical world. And apart from his technical skills, he had the ability to show care and engender trust. What a great combination brains, skill, and a heart! How could I not love him?

Ten

As time moved forward, the problems with my body receded into the background and I was able to concentrate on our family. Ten years after the birth of our first grandchild, Lauren, we welcomed sweet Julia. A year later, Master Dylan arrived, and then eight months after that we were blessed with little Grace. Only one month later there was Katherine, and as of this writing, the last (and of course not least) is dear, precious Matthew. Five grandchildren in four years and then there were six. It is as though all the joy was piled into one short period of life, just tumbling towards us, making up for the misery of the past. How lucky we are to have two of our children living nearby so that we can be involved with their children. Unfortunately John and Joan live too far away for us have that level of daily contact, but when we do get together, it is valuable and memorable.

Though there was drama aplenty in my medical life I managed to maintain a slow but steady, upward-mobility professional career. I had started working when I was fifteen, doing part-time secretarial work for a local land surveyor. I stayed with him until I graduated high school, when I left for full time work. After attempts at several different jobs I finally landed what would be a life-saving position, one that would provide support for me through all of the trials that lay ahead.

I started as a typist at the Foundation for Christian Living. When I left in 1992, I was a multi-department manager in charge of a staff of about 50. Landing this job was proof once again that for some of it, I was in the right place at the right time. The foundation was a small non-profit organization with its roots in Christianity. It was also something of a good old boys' club when I first arrived and while that was not too appealing, there was a positive element to it. The guys felt a need to "take care" of the women.

I was employed with this organization when I was going through some of my most difficult life situations. My co-workers supported my efforts to survive and, at the same time, allowed me to move forward in my career. I continued taking college courses, and during that time, I represented the organization at conferences and spoke at gatherings. I was in the company of notable people, such as Max Cleland, Elizabeth Dole, and our organization's founder, the wonderful Dr. Norman Vincent Peale.

When the foundation offered me a buyout in 1992, I think my colleagues were shocked when I took it. I was in my 40s, much younger than the other employees who were accepting this offer, but I felt it was time to leave. I had been remarried for a few years now I had the support and security I needed at home. I felt grounded enough to try something new and so I left and went on to the next chapter of life.

About the time I was considering retiring from the foundation my husband learned he had 13 half-brothers and sisters. Just six weeks before our marriage and the sudden death of his mother, Joe learned the name of his biological father. This opened a new portal for him through which he would start a search for the rest of his family. Unlike me, Joe was surrounded by a strong family unit. He and his mother had lived with his grandfather and usually an aunt and her children, while her husband was serving in the military. As I watched him diligently pursue these family members, I was inspired to try and find my own scattered siblings. The six of us had never all been in the same room at the same time. As a matter of fact, I later found out that the younger ones did not know we even existed.

I started my search for my siblings by writing to the county clerk's office in Montgomery Alabama for the marriage license of my sister Pauline. I had a vague memory of Pauline's father taking her to Alabama and a letter from my mother that had been postmarked Montgomery, Alabama. I figured by now she could be married. I was right. Within a few days, I was standing in my kitchen looking at a copy of her marriage license, from which I learned her married name. The rest was easy. I called information in the town listed on the certificate Pell City, Alabama and asked for her phone number. I was partly lucky I got the number of her sister-in-law, Charlotte. That evening I called and after I explained who I was, Charlotte gave me Pauline's number. As I prepared to call Pauline, I was filled with anticipation, fear and the dreaded thought of rejection. How could I be sure she would be interested in speaking with me? But then I thought, *I have come this far and I have to make this call.*

When I called Pauline's house, I was greeted by a voice on the other end with a very, very southern accent. It was her daughter Stephanie. As with Charlotte, I explained who I was, and the young girl cried out,

"You mean my momma's got kin?" I hoped this was good news for her.

But Pauline was not at home. Without leaving my number, I told Stephanie I would call back at 9 a.m. the next day. Too bad, I was not thinking! I later learned that when Pauline heard the news of my call, she was unable to sleep all night. Well, I did call back, and when she answered the phone, it was just as wonderful to hear her voice as I had imagined it would be.

"Hi Pauline, this is your big sister Joanne."

"Oh my word, I can't believe I am talking to you, I can't believe I have a sister."

"Well my dear you have three sisters and two brothers." There was silence on the other end of the phone.

"And by the way, your mother is alive." Again there was silence on the other end of the phone.

"Pauline, are you there?" I could only imagine what was going through her head. Here she was living her life and then receives a call like this. I know for me I felt like my head was going to explode along with my heart.

"Yes, I am Joanne. When I was left in the orphanage I was told I was an only child and my mother had died in childbirth."

"Well, none of that is true," I said.

"You have lots of family and I am going to get us all together. I will Pauline. Trust me. I will make it happen." She sounded overwhelmed and ecstatic all at the same time.

"Promise Joanne you can do this," she said.

"Yes, I can and I will." As the conversation continued we talked about how many children we had, where we lived and about our respective marriages. I told her what I could without overloading her on our first conversation. Before I hung up the phone I promised I would call her once a week and keep her posted on the progress of our family reunion which would take place at my home later that year.

Joe and I made arrangements to visit my brother John in Florida and thought that would be a good opportunity to meet up with Pauline, who would come and find me in the Atlanta airport. John and I had been in contact off and on since he returned from the Navy. At the time of my search, he had settled in Florida.

Joe and I flew down from New York and when we made the stopover in Atlanta we looked around for Pauline. Perhaps she was looking for me too, but of course, neither one of us knew what the other looked like. The time was getting close for us to board our flight and I didn't want to miss the chance to see Pauline before leaving for Florida, but it seemed she left me no choice.

But then, just as Joe and I were about to board the plane, I heard a very southern voice.

"Joanne" my sister called to me. I turned to see Pauline walking toward me. She was a tall woman with a head of bushy blond hair, cut short, like mine. We embraced and took a few moments to just feel the beauty of the experience. Someone in Pauline's husband's family had called a local Atlanta TV station and they caught it all on tape and we were on the local Atlanta news that night. Then, being practical we quickly found a place to sit and talk before they made the last call for our flight.

Our conversation was a blur of questions.

"How many kids did you have?" I asked.

"Will we ever see each other again?" she said. I was saddened to hear that Pauline had not been able to turn around her life of hardship. As a young child, she had been placed in an orphanage. She was told that she was an only child whose mother had died in childbirth. When she left the orphanage upon graduating from high school, she made one bad decision after another just as I had. Pell City is a very depressed area with few opportunities for success. She should have left, but instead. Pauline married, had three children and worked in the seafood department of the local grocery store to keep food on the table. And it turns out Pauline had never met her Joe, as I had.

In this short visit, it was impossible to even begin to learn much about each other but it was painfully obvious to me by Pauline's demeanor that there was a lot more to learn about her and her life. I felt I had made contact with a bright, intelligent woman with a heart of gold, who had never taken that next step to make her life move forward. I can only surmise that Pauline, like all of us, needed to learn to love herself first.

Our meeting was short and we talked until they were about to shut the door of the plane.

"I am going to make arrangements to bring you to New York," I told her.

"Then we can have that long-awaited family gathering." Pauline could hardly contain her joy. Then it was time to say goodbye. When Joe and I boarded the plane, I was emotionally exhausted from the visit, filled with so many thoughts and questions about Pauline and her life. But there would be time later to get to know my sister better.

Upon arrival in Florida we rented a car, and drove to my brother John's home. We had a great visit and most of the conversation was about our visit with Pauline. I had told John that I was going to meet Pauline at the airport; however I was not sure he believed it would happen.

"How did she know you?" John asked. I told him I'd described myself as a tall blond and that I'd be wearing a red leather jacket.

"So you were the only blond in the Atlanta airport with a red leather jacket on?" "Well no I also told her that I would be with Joe who was 6ft. 6in. tall. Very easy to spot us, don't you think. I told her the gate we'd be waiting at."

"What does she look like?"

"She is tall, about 5ft. 9in. and a crop of curly blond hair. Remember like she did as a little girl." John just sat back on the couch and lifted his cup of coffee to take a sip.

"Wow, I can hardly believe you are pulling this together." I reviewed with John the idea of a family reunion; he was delighted with the thought and assured me he would be there.

As soon as Joe and I got home from Florida, I began my search for Jamie. I knew that Jamie had been adopted by a family in Peekskill, New York, and was going on the hunch that she might still be in the area. I looked in the phone book for her adoptive parents, whose name was Westfall. The last time I visited Jamie she was about 12 years old, the beginning of difficult years for young people. My son had just been born and I wanted to share this special event with my little sister. Gerry and I took a trip to Verplank, New York to visit our little sister and introduce her to her new nephew. When we arrived 12 year-old Jamie was waiting on the porch to greet us.

"Wow, what a cute baby can I hold him?" She asked.

"Sure, I said but I think it would be better if you sit down first." Sit she did and I handed over my son her nephew. But the visit did not go as well as we had hoped. Jamie had her own life and that life did not include us. Adding another dimension to her life would not be fair. Jamie was a happy and seemingly well adjusted 12-year old. She had a family that loved her and a circle of school friends. It seemed clear to us by her reception of us that she really didn't need this distraction in her life. Quite frankly she was almost a teenager and quite self absorbed. Don't get me wrong she was pleasant and excited to see us. She lived in a comfortable home with her adoptive mom and dad and she had two adoptive sisters. She was a happy kid and very polite but more interested in meeting her friends after we left to catch a movie. You know that age is difficult and pre-teens are not really in anything but the here and now. Gerry and I both thought it better to step back and let Jamie make the next move if she wanted, but we did not hear from her again.

But now almost 25 years had gone by and I wanted to reconnect with her. I called the only Westfall that was listed in the book; that call put me in touch with a man who turned out to be Jamie's uncle. After I explained who I was and what the purpose of my call was he gave me a number where I could reach Jamie's adoptive mother. Finally in touch with Mrs. Westfall, I found myself quite nervous and could hear myself rattling on and on. She listened silently at first.

"I can't believe this," she said.

"Jamie and I were talking about you just the other day!" I breathed a sigh of relief into the phone.

"She's been trying to find you for years," Mrs. Westfall explained they had moved when Jamie was 13 and they'd lost my address.

"Jamie didn't remember your married name," the woman said. She promised to have Jamie call me as soon as she could and sure enough just a little while later, my phone rang. My hand was trembling as I pick up the phone.

"Hello."

"Is that you Joanne?"

"Yes it is Jamie," how are you?"

"I can't believe it was so easy to find you, just one phone call." She still sounded like that 12-year old little girl. Her voice was soft and gentle. For a moment I was transported back in time, and it was wonderful. I shook myself back to reality and Jamie continued.

"Joanne, my mother and I have been trying to contact you for several years with no luck." Her voice cracked and it sounded like she was crying.

"I know Jamie your mom told me." I played the big sister role and assured her this was the beginning of a new time for us.

"Joanne, I am so glad you found me, glad we found each other. I was just about to give up hope of ever finding you." We talked for a long time about our lives. Jamie, now divorced, had three children, Melissa, Rebecca and John. She was working as a waitress and like Pauline was trying to hold things together. This made me very sad. It also made me feel so blessed that I had managed to get my act together. As I hung up I wished that Jamie would have better days ahead.

I called Gerry to tell her I had found Jamie and the three of us met the following evening at the diner where Jamie was working. Gerry and I walked into the diner which seemed quite empty. Standing by the counter was a woman who looked a lot like Gerry and my mother.

"Joanne?" I ran to Jamie and gave her a big hug and she even commented on how she looked like Gerry. She was thin with reddish-blond hair, wearing red and so was I. She then turned to the other female standing by the counter and introduced her.

"Melissa, I would like you to meet my older sisters Joanne and Gerry.

"Hi Aunt Joanne, hi Aunt Gerry" my niece responded in a shy voice. We all sat down in a booth and began to catch up on each other's lives. Gerry and I told Jamie about our lives, our children and work. The rattle of dishes and silverware in the background played like the musical accompaniment to our conversation. The waitresses and customers were the cast in this long-awaited reunion scene. As we sat in the booth chattering it seemed to us we were the only people in the diner. We were so excited that we just rambled on and on, seemingly for hours. There were lots of tears and laughter and as the evening ended we embraced, it seemed as if letting go of one another might separate us forever. We did not want that to happen.

"You promise?" Jamie asked as we all headed for the parking lot.

"Promise we will see each other again?" We were all adults now and knew that we needed each other.

"Yes, Jamie," I said.

"I promise we will see each other again. You can count on that."

"Okay big sister I will hold you to that."

"Don't worry" Gerry said.

"If Joanne says it will happen you can count on that," Gerry added.

"Believe me I know."

Later in the week, Ronnie drove from Long Island to Westchester to meet his youngest sister, Jamie. They met at the same diner where we had our reunion, but their meeting was different. It was extremely emotional because neither of them knew the other had existed. Ronnie wanted to know everything about Jamie's life and, of course, she wanted to know about him. They talked about their kids, their work, and other general topics, but they talked about the amazement of the meeting. For long periods of time they just stared at each other, emotions running high and tears flowing easily. They each said they would never forget this event. Jamie's later reunion with Mother, Pauline, and John would have to wait until the summer.

It is Sunday and I am in the kitchen doing what I do every Sunday making sauce. As I stir the pot I realize I have stirred the pot of life for my siblings. Gathering everyone together was both exciting and scary. We don't know Pauline or Jamie. Would the reunion be a positive happening? I couldn't imagine any other outcome.

"Ouch!" As the sauce comes to a boil and splatters my arm. I shake myself back to reality and the task at hand. After all, the kids and our granddaughter would be here soon for Sunday sauce.

John, Gerry and I had always been together but the rest of the family was scattered. Looking back I see that Ronnie had the most difficult life of all. After the fire he was placed in Kings Park, a home for delinquent boys and we never heard from him until he was about to get married. In that holding place, where he spent about ten years, he was pretty much treated like a prisoner. As adults, when Ron and I talked about our past, he shared bits and pieces of his time spent in Kings Park.

"It was a hell hole not fit for animals," he said.

"Joanne, I can't talk about it. I get so furious about what they did to me I could kill those bastards that worked in that place." Emotions would run high when he talked of the degradation and abuse. When he finally got out, he lived a tough street life in New York and Long Island and eventually met and married his first wife, Jean. They lived in Long Island and had five children. But in time, the marriage did not work out and Ronnie moved on.

I did learn that before he married, Ronnie made it his mission to find his sisters. When he started his search, he only knew about John, Gerry and me but had no knowledge of Pauline and Jamie. I knew these girls existed. Ron only learned about Pauline and Jamie from me as I prepared for our awesome family reunion.

For a long time, whenever anyone asked about my family, I found it was easier to just say I had two brothers and a sister and didn't mention Pauline and Jamie. But I never forgot about them; I thought of them as my two "lost" sisters. When I was younger I would fantasize that they were both healthy, happy and wore frilly dresses with bows on them. Somehow that seemed to make it a little better. For nearly 40 years, every holiday and family occasion brought with it the painful reminder that our family was incomplete.

Well, all my hard work would eventually pay off. I worked for months making sure every detail was covered the guest list, food, beverages. Had I remembered everything? Did we have enough chairs? Oh my God the weather! I even took responsibility for that.

The day of our family reunion arrived. It was a hot, hazy, Saturday afternoon in July 1990, when my mother, my two brothers, and all three of my sisters gathered at our home. Joe and I were both excited and nervous when we greeted our guests. This was no ordinary backyard barbecue this was a day I'd dreamed about all my life. Our home was filled with over 50 friends and family who gathered to meet everyone and support us in this very big event in our lives. Here came Bonnie and Ray, my foster mother's granddaughter and her husband. Just behind them was Bonnie and Ray's daughter Tracy. Kisses and hugs were shared by all. The excitement was infectious and our guests were genuinely happy for our family. Oh, here comes my son Everett with his wife Debbie carrying our beautiful granddaughter Lauren, not quite a year old. As I darted around greeting folks, Joe was making sure all the details we discussed were being taken care of. What a day! Photos were snapped, stories told and there were lots of tears and laughter. As the day came to an end, a gentle rain began to fall. We were all outside with music playing and found ourselves dancing to the very vibrant song "We Are Family."

As I looked around my eyes filled with tears. Dreams do come true! I was standing there watching my dream come to life. We were all together at last. I was amazed at my mother's behavior. There she was for the first time ever with all her children and you would think it were a day like any other. She acted like this happened every weekend, just another family get-together at one of her children's homes. The fact of the matter was that she really didn't know any of them that well and Jamie and Pauline she knew nothing about them except what she had learned in the last few months. She was the proud mother greeting the guests and accepting their compliments about her family. I truly believe she had spent her whole life waiting for this moment, however, when it came it was just another day for her to be the center of attention. I think this was a much more meaningful event for the siblings than it was for our mother. We were all overwhelmed with emotion and joy, thankful for the events of the day.

After this event our lives were forever altered. Never would there be a holiday or family occasion when I wouldn't think of the day we were all together. We knew then we would not always be together for celebrations and events, but we were truly a family.

As years passed it seemed as if we would never again be in the same place at the same time, but as we approached the wedding of my brother John, it looked as if five out of the six siblings would be there. But our reunion would always be a hard act to follow.

The next day we all gathered for a brunch at our house. Somehow the mood had changed, especially for Ron. We were all sitting in the living room and Ron began his interrogations. First to Jamie and Pauline, why did you not try to find us? Pauline said she did not know that we existed and Jamie said she did without success. Then it was our mothers turn. Ron asked why she had thrown her kids to the wind, why. Why? I just want to know why. The silence was deafening and she said nothing. Ron said all he ever wanted was an apology.

"I just wanted to hear you say you were sorry," he said.

John, Gerry and I were in and out of the room all of us with tears in our eyes. Then mom got up and walked out of the room and then back in.

"I'm sorry" she said and proceeded to go to each of us and kiss us and repeat her apology. That was it, it was over 45+ years of abandonment and that's what we got an, I'm sorry! But then that's all Ron had asked for. And really what more could she say?

Eleven

After accepting that early buyout from my company, I decided to take some time and do a few of the things I had always wanted to do. I got very involved in power-walking and got into top shape. It felt so good to be healthy mentally, emotionally and physically.

We had been invited to visit Joe's cousin in England and from there we took a trip to Ireland. Joe's cousin's husband was in the travel business and arranged the excursion for us.

On my father's side of the family, I am of Irish descent. All of my father's brothers and his sister were born in Ireland. What made this trip so exciting was that I was able to locate, I believe, the last living member of the Keane family in Ireland my father's cousin, Tom Keane. We also visited the cemetery where family members were buried and walked around the Keane family home. Joe and I took Tom Keane to lunch in a nearby town and he was so proud to tell his friends that his family from America had come to visit him. Tom called the bartender over.

"Hey Roy, my great niece from America came to have lunch with me." I reached out to shake the man's hand. We ordered lunch and Tom got a grilled cheese sandwich. Tom was dressed in a sport jacket and a snap cap. As we sat in the pub and ate lunch and chatted, Tom told us about his work in the church and about his brother's death a few months earlier. Telling this story made him very sad. When we were ready to leave I watched Tom wrap the uneaten half of his grilled cheese sandwich in a napkin and put it in his pocket.

"Tom, can we go next door and get a few things for you?" I asked. Next door was a small deli.

"No matter to me. If you wish do so." We went next door to the deli and purchased some fruit, cookies and a jug of juice. He was thrilled.

At the end of the day, Tom asked us if we could visit again the following month and more often if possible! Tom was a simple man, a caretaker for the church, who did not really understand that monthly trips were not very likely. When I returned home though, I began corresponding with him. Tom only wrote in Gaelic, so his neighbor translated my letters to him and she wrote letters to me that Tom dictated. I felt for the very first time a connection with my father's family.

But even more rewarding than our travel adventures was the fact that I was now able to care for our granddaughter, Lauren. I watched her a few days a week and enrolled her in nursery school, becoming a *nursery school mom*. This was a role I had never been able to enjoy with my son and it was just as wonderful as I had imagined it would be.

I also had more time to volunteer for activities with organizations like the American Cancer Society and giving support to single, divorced, and separated women. I got interested in Literacy Volunteers of America and went through the two-week program, which instructed volunteers how to teach folks to write and read English.

As a literacy graduate, I was contacted by the New York State Department of Youth to help young offenders get their GEDs. These were kids just like my siblings and me, but they had prison sentences to serve for substance abuse, murder and many other problems. I was fortunate enough to help several young people in the program attain their goal of getting their GED. I especially remember one young man who was serving a sentence for murder, though this young man was only 14 years old. As his 15th birthday approached, I asked about the possibility of having a birthday party for Jose. After much discussion our birthday party was approved. Jose was allowed to invite another inmate from his cell block. I brought pizza, soda and gifts. It was so gratifying for me. It brought me back to that first Christmas at my foster home. I knew how he felt when he opened his gifts. I truly believe this was the first birthday celebration he had ever had and perhaps the first time he had unwrapped a gift. I understood his joy and left feeling I had made a difference in his life. Several weeks later he was being released and I often wondered if he was living a good life. I can't help but wonder how different my life and the lives of my siblings might have been if someone had been there early on to support and encourage us.

With extra time on my hands that summer, I was able to find more and more ways to give back to my community. I was always looking for opportunities to help one more person make it through the darkness that life can be. Through the Literacy Volunteer program I took up the cause to help a young immigrant woman named Rosa acquire survival skills to function in everyday life here in the U. S. Rosa and I shopped at the local supermarket, prepared meals together and went to the mall to shop for personal items. I did not exactly follow the program guidelines, but felt that I was giving Rosa the tools she needed to function independently. My tutelage for Rosa took place about ten years ago and every Christmas I get a card from her, with pictures of her children. What's particularly touching is that Rosa makes those cards on a computer. When I met her, not only could she not use a computer, she could not even say computer! Several years later, Rosa was diagnosed with a breast lump and called me for support. I was more than happy to accompany her to her doctor's appointments and her biopsy, which turned out to be benign. I was so privileged to be there for her.

I spent my summer in meaningful ways and had something to show for it. When fall arrived and Lauren was ready to go to kindergarten, I decided to return to work. My granddaughter no longer needed a babysitter and it was clear that another stage of life was beginning, though I was not quite sure what that would entail.

When I thought about going back to work, I had to consider that I was now fifty-one and had been out of the working game for almost two years. In addition, most of my experience had been with one organization over a period of twenty-five years. The best approach, I thought, would be to start with a temp agency. I did not want a position with any responsibility. Certainly I had had a lot of that my whole life and wasn't in search of recognition or prestige. I took a position as a receptionist at an office rental company. I loved it. I just answered the phone, transferred calls and took messages. Then the boss went on vacation and left me in charge, it did not take long for the right person to notice my working style. I was soon promoted to office manager, which naturally put me once again in the position of being *in charge*, exactly what I'd been avoiding. But then, as happens in many job scenarios of this kind, the boss was threatened by my competence (still a problem for women in the business arena, whether their boss is a man or a woman). My boss went on vacation and left me in charge. We had hired a temporary employee from an agency to do power point presentations for the clients. I had been observing this employee over a couple of days and noticed she spent a lot of time taking breaks and going to the parking garage where her car was parked. Just after the afternoon break she returned to the office and I thought she was acting a bit inappropriate and when I approached her I could smell alcohol on her breath. When I asked her if she had been drinking she stared at me.

"Oh no, not me," she said.

"Well, what did you have to eat? Your breath smells like alcohol." She starred at me and slowly stood up and then sat quickly. She was swaying back and forth in her chair. I asked her again. I expected she would fall off the chair any minute.

"Have you been drinking?"

"Well just a swig, not too much." I proceeded to call the agency and sent her back. They understood, however, my boss saw it as a threat. Before long, I was laid off. This had been my first taste of corporate America. It was bittersweet in that it was exciting and challenging, but certainly nothing like the caring, people-first environment of the non-profit world.

I soon landed a position with a client from the job I had just left. John, the president of Brandywine Retained Ventures, Inc., an executive search firm, had been watching me in action. He had decided that if I were ever available, he'd want to use my experience to bring some stability to his young staff. But he made a poor choice in hiring me as a recruiter. I hated it and I had no training. Quite frankly, I got very tired of potential candidates hanging up on me. It wasn't long before I told John I planned to leave. I explained to him that I really was not comfortable cold calling and was afraid I was doing more harm than good to his list of possible candidates. John was not happy with my news and told me I could choose any job in the company that I wanted. He said he valued my maturity and business expertise. His current staff consisted of a group of very young folks with little experience. At this time I felt that what he really needed for his staff was a mother and I was not about to sign up for that job.

But john would not hear of my leaving.

"What would it take for you to stay?" he asked.

"I just want to be the receptionist. You don't have one and in a position like that, I will be able to familiarize myself with the clients and the business."

"Agreed," he said.

Soon after becoming receptionist, I was promoted to office manager. I became more familiar with the day-to-day operations and was soon offering suggestions for streamlining the business. Then after less than one year as office manager, I was promoted to director of operations. With this step up, I was delighted and validated for all my hard work and dedication and soon realized I knew nothing else but being in a position of responsibility. After all I had been in charge since I was about three years old. It was clear that in the corporate world, career growth was much faster than in the non-profit world.

As our business grew, our staff increased and so did our management problems. It was soon apparent that John needed to concern himself with growing the business and let someone else take total responsibility for the operation. And so I was promoted to chief operating officer. With this promotion and the added responsibilities, the stress level increased dramatically. I represented the company at conferences, giving lectures on salary and compensation for recruiters, and sat on panels to debate such issue.

It was now 2000, and the executive search business was very much in demand. The trend was slowly changing and corporations seemed to feel more secure using the larger companies for their searches. John, who had earned an excellent reputation by now, was convinced he wanted to be hired by a major search firm and I would come along as part of the deal. I was now offered my dream job and having run a search firm and learned the business, I was primed for the challenge. I was working from home and only traveled into the city for an occasional meeting. I was doing what I wanted, had plenty of freedom and was making terrific money. I had arrived, so I thought.

I loved working from home. I was able to interview candidates and do laundry at the same time. However, one day as I walked upstairs with the laundry, I found myself needing to sit and catch my breath. I was concerned because I considered myself to be in good shape and wondered what this could be. Joe and I walked four to six miles a day and were very active grandparents but there was obviously a problem.

As I tried to figure out the breathing situation, I was faced with an additional problem, chest pain. I finally got up the courage to go to the doctor. When I described the symptoms, he referred me to a cardiologist for a stress test.

I failed. The doctor immediately stopped the treadmill and gave me a bottle of nitroglycerin tablets. Of course, he scheduled me for additional tests which revealed that I had a congenital condition called myocardial bridging, which, in layman's terms, means that the large artery, the LAD, which crosses over the top of the heart, dips into my heart and with every beat, squeezes the artery. And if this occurs every time your heart beats, after fifty plus years, you've got a problem.

"What do I do?" I asked the doctor. He told me that to keep this condition in check; I would need to remove stress from my life. There was to be no more heavy lifting! Well isn't that just great? Overnight I became an invalid at least I felt like one. I could not allow my heart rate to exceed one hundred ten. I could not run and play with my grandchildren or pick them up and my family began to watch me like a hawk. If I followed these instructions and took a daily medication for the rest of my life, I could keep this condition under control. I was overwhelmed, knowing that this would change every part of my personal and professional life.

And just at that time, when this health problem arose, that absolutely perfect job I had was about to explode right in my face. The company decided that they needed to cut costs, and to this end, they would no longer use outside consultants like me. This was confusing and upsetting. I had just been told I was doing a great job!

I called the company to ask what could be done and was told that there was a place for me in the New York office. This was just what I did not need and did not want: a daily commute by train to Manhattan, rushing through Grand Central, carrying a laptop, a briefcase and running between appointments. With that, my consulting career ended as quickly as it began. It was great while it lasted and now it was over. That kind of stress would not be what the doctor had ordered for me. I was devastated. I had been doing what I loved and Joe was now retired, which meant most nights when I arrived home Joe would meet me at the door and we would enjoy a glass of wine before he would serve dinner. Life was good and he was so proud and happy for me. He would often tell me that he was so pleased I finally got a chance to show the world how capable I was. He has always been my champion!

Realizing my life was taking a quieter turn I did what I always did, I accepted whatever lay ahead for me and was determined to make the best of it.

Twelve

When people hear my story, they often ask, "How did you get through all that stuff in your life?" As you can see, *getting through* took a lot of fortitude and a core belief that life *could* be better. I suppose I can take credit for some of this thinking, but I really could not have gotten through what life dealt me without my experience at the Foundation for Christian Living. I was just twenty-two when I started. At the time, I realized we would have to pay my son's exorbitant hospital bills and I would need to find work. My former mother-in-law worked at the foundation and used her influence to land me an interview. I worked as a typist for two years and then became secretary to the executive editor, Myron L. Boardman. Eventually I left for a better job elsewhere. When my son was ready to attend school I realized I would need to be closer to his school. One afternoon Mr. Boardman called me at my new job and asked if I would consider coming back to the Foundation, this time as a supervisor. I thought I played it cool and told him I would think about it. The foundation was less than an eighth of a mile from my son's school. Was that great or what? I called Mr. Boardman and told him I would take the job. Once again timing was everything. It was not the job that was important as much as the organization itself, which was always rooted in the practice of positive thinking.

The co-founder and leader of this organization was Dr. Norman Vincent Peale, author of *The Power of Positive Thinking*. I was privileged to have a personal relationship with Dr. Peale and his wife, Ruth in my more than 25-year career at this organization. Every day during those years and since, I've tried to put the Dr. Peale values into practice. He was a man who practiced what he preached. He was humble and treated everyone with respect. After I was privileged to witness these principals work so well in the lives of others, I learned to think positively about my own life.

Having a leadership role in the Peale organization was key in changing my life. My job influenced the way I lived my life and impacted what I thought about myself, how I conducted my life within the organization and in the world at large.

By the time I was considering divorce I was the operations manager, supervising four departments and a staff of approximately fifty. At this church-based organization, divorce was frowned upon. I had mixed feelings about dissolving my marriage and I brought my concerns to Dr. Peale. He listened, counseled me and told me about his belief in his marriage vows. He advised me to consider my twenty years of marriage and not just the bad times. If the bad times outweighed the good and I still felt this was the best decision for me he would support any choice I would make. And he did. Dr. Peale was a wonderful man. He was like a surrogate father to me.

One day Joe stopped by the office for coffee. He had been a guidance counselor in the neighboring town where he had counseled many of the employee's children. When he arrived in the break room many of the women began to praise him and talk about what a wonderful person he was and how he had helped their families. Well Dr. Peale listened to just about enough of that talk and announced to Joe and those at our table,

"Well, let me tell you about Joanne and what a great contribution she has made to this organization." Joe tells that story still today. He always says Dr. Peale would not let the women praise him without defending my worth.

The power of positive thinking and the organization's practice of same, certainly made the difficult times of my life more manageable. When I was recovering from surgery I missed many days of work, but the organization never withheld my paycheck. It would be the same when I needed chemotherapy treatments or had doctor appointments. God bless the Foundation for Christian Living; (now the Peale Center for Christian Living) they stood by me all the way.

If I were to sum up all the problems I had during those years, the list would be long: multiple medical crises, cancer, living with an abusive alcoholic husband, and then our inevitable divorce. But regardless of what I was going through, I always tried to maintain a professional demeanor to be a motivating force and productive member of the executive staff within the organization. My belief in the principles of positive thinking made it possible for me to more than survive those difficult years. I learned to survive and thrive. I woke every morning and listed all that was *good* in my life. For starters I gave *thanks* for waking up. Then I went to work, refusing to let negativity get the upper hand in my life. I am a living testimony that positive thinking really does work!

Thirteen

Just as my own life was getting to somewhat normal, my mother died. The day she passed away was filled with drama. It was a Saturday night when the phone rang and my mother's caretaker, Delta, was on the line.

Delta was really more than a caretaker; she was also my mother's friend and somewhat of a buffer between my mother and me. They had met when they worked together at M J's Ice Cream Shop. Throughout her life, when there wasn't a man around to support her, my mother would get a clerking job. She had intermittent jobs in places like S. H. Kress, Tiffany's and other retail stores in Manhattan. When she got older and moved to Tennessee with her ailing second husband, she became a hardworking woman who took her work seriously. She was still rough around the edges. She would yell at the employees in the ice cream shop, make them feel bad and then expect them to step up to the plate and get the job done. Even though she was just a clerk, because of her age and demeanor, the younger employees were afraid of her. She had no real authority but that didn't seem to matter. At times she was crude in her interaction with her co-workers, somehow believing that the boss would like her take-charge posture. Most of the employees were much younger than mom. One day I was at the shop when a young employee came in late.

"You get in that kitchen and hurry up about it." She would bellow as she scooped ice cream into a cone.

"Yes I'll get right at it," the young girl replied.

"You bet you will or I'll tell Mr. T you were late." Then she would turn to a customer as if she had done something great. If one of them would sit for a minute she would yell at them with a shop full of customers and tell them to get out there and clear a table, or fill the napkin holder. They were afraid of her. But then workers would quit, leaving the owner of the ice cream shop to find new help, most often at an increased hourly wage.

Mom lived life her way and anyone who did not agree with her was wrong. Delta, however, was that one person who was able to work with her. Delta had lost her mother at an early age and may have been looking for a mother figure, which amazingly, mom managed to be for her. In a sense, she adopted mom. However, I think Delta did more of the mothering than mom did.

Somehow, they were good for each other. Mom filled a void in Delta's life and absolutely, Delta filled a void in mom's life. Delta was the daughter who didn't know the truth about mom, who managed to escape those early terrible years. Unlike me she could be that loving, giving daughter who accepted mom unconditionally. In time, they formed a strong bond and truly loved each other. When mom would call me, she always talked about Delta. I did not know her and quite frankly I didn't really care, but I was grateful that Delta was taking some of the burden of caretaking off my shoulders. I was not anxious, however, to become her friend.

I later learned that Delta was an *angel in disguise*. She took mom to her doctor appointments and saw she took the right amount of medication and ate properly. Eventually she moved mom into her home. As the daughter on the outside looking in, I had to admit that it couldn't get any better than that. And soon Delta became my friend as well. I learned she was a person of great depth and love for her fellow human beings, a religious woman who practiced what she preached. True, sincere and solid, she was a godsend for mom and for all of us. It was truly a gift that Delta allowed mom to move in with her because as far as I was concerned she had *nursing home stamped on her forehead*!

That night when the call came, I knew something had to be wrong.

"It's mom, Joanne," she said.

"I need you to make a decision. She is dying and I need to know if you want the paramedics to resuscitate her." Damn, I was so angry!

Even on her deathbed my mother put me on the spot. All I could think was, *I have to make the decision, why not call Ronnie, Gerry? Anyone but me!* I could hear the paramedics in the background.

Suddenly, I told Delta,

"No, mom has a DNR. Do not resuscitate!" I was mom's power of attorney and realized the only one who could make that decision. Then my next thought was, *OK, you did it. You gave them permission to let her die.* I hated to be the one to decide, but it was done now.

Some time before, we discovered that mom had moved in with Delta and was not living in the house that Joe and I had bought from her. Our decision to sell was a difficult decision. Joe and I had taken over mom's mortgage and had spent many hours and a great deal of money keeping the house in livable condition. In those last years before mom moved out, she did little or nothing to help keep the house up. Like some older people, she became increasingly difficult to deal with too, and the whole long-distance thing became more than we could or wanted to manage.

It took eleven days to get the house ready to sell. It was filthy and cluttered, and the stench was unbearable. *Why,* I asked myself, *would she do this to the home she loved? And why would she do this to us?* Joe and I would visit often and when we did he would fix everything that needed repair. We were the only ones who took the time to help on a regular basis. Was this the thanks we got? Then my light bulb moment: she only cared for herself and for people or things that mattered to her. I was obviously not one of those people. Since I was not willing to be her subservient daughter any longer she turned on me and my husband. She quickly forgot the generosity that had allowed her to stay in the house for so many years She forgot who paid for the repairs and who did most of those repairs, me and Joe.

Mom had already moved out by the time we took a ride to assess what needed to be done. We arrived at the house intending to address all kinds of issues everything from repairs to painting, to emptying the property of its contents. When we opened the front door, the horrid odor and mountains of clutter literally made us physically ill. As we perused the mess, we noted that mom had taken anything we might need to make a meal; the bed was piled high with junk and there wasn't even toilet tissue in the bathroom. Curtain rods were pulled off the walls, not removed just pulled out. Piles of dirty clothes were piled on chairs and couches. We did all we needed to get through the first night and retired for a greatly needed rest. We talked about why mom may have done this.

"I think it is because she is accustomed to getting her way and we were not letting that happen," I said.

"I think you are right, however the fact remains what she did was so wrong."

"I just don't get it Joe," I said.

"She loved this place but the devastation she left here is, I think, how she feels about us." I pulled the dirty clothes off the bed in the guest room so I could prepare a place for us to sleep. Joe got a sheet from our truck to put on the bed.

"Don't worry about it tonight. Maybe things will look better in the morning."

Morning did not bring the relief we might have expected or hoped for. As we arose, we were still baffled as to why mom had done this. When I asked her the next day, she denied any involvement and blamed Delta! Why had I bothered to ask? Mom has never taken responsibility for her actions.

So we began the arduous task of cleaning up this incredible mess. It took us 11 days, working 10 to 12 hours a day, cleaning, packing and getting rid of the accumulation of about 15 years. After the cleanup, we began having the house painted and preparing the house for sale. It was difficult and exhausting. Nothing about this was pleasant, either physically or emotionally.

Mom wasn't living too far away, so every day she would come by and just sit and watch us work. We would ask her about things she might want to save and she would just stare at us, as if we were doing something wrong. I became so distressed.

"Mom, what do you want us to do? Do you want to stay in the house, which has been empty for over a year?"

"No," she replied.

"I am where I want to be." We could not help but think that she disapproved of our decision to sell the house. I guess she wanted to keep it for her personal storage unit.

When all the work was done and it was a huge project we swung by Delta's to say goodbye. We received a rather chilly reception from mom, but Delta was her usually chatty and pleasant self. Mom talked about her friend whose daughter had given her part of the proceeds of the sale of her home, saying what a good daughter she had been. There was not much point in using logic here, but I did remind her that we had paid for this house and took financial responsibility for all its repairs. It was no use, though. I learned later that she tried to contact a lawyer in hopes of suing us! I was stunned, not to mention the extreme hurt. When Joe and I took over her house, mom was out of money and could not meet the mortgage payments. And although it had not been a goal for us to make money, it turned out that in our efforts to help mom live a little more comfortably, we actually lost money. Well, so much for good deeds. But, really why was I surprised at my mother's response? She had been behaving this way her whole life. It was always about her. How silly of us to think she might be even slightly grateful for us bailing her out and giving her the opportunity to live out her life in the home she loved.

Four months later, as I stood gazing at mom in her casket, like everyone else, I was a bit emotional. But it was difficult to understand where those emotions came from. I suppose I had mixed feelings about my mother's passing after all. It was especially difficult for me since I had spent much more time with her than did my siblings those last few years. I looked at the woman who was my mother and felt dismayed. She would never get Mother of the Year award but she did give us life and deserves something for that. Then I looked at my brother Ronnie. He was weeping and I really could not understand that at all. He got the worst of mom but he appeared to be the most affected. I believe he never came to grips with the impact mom had on his life. It would be so very painful for him to really face that and know the full effect. No one can help Ron with that. He will have to address that himself.

As I watched all the folks wander into the funeral home, I asked myself what they knew about my mother that I did not. They filed past her casket as if she were royalty, tears running down their faces, whispering to us what a loss she will be to the community. During the actual funeral, strangers spoke of mom's *goodness* and her contributions to life. I sat there thinking, *I am the eldest daughter and I probably should get up and say something*. But I had nothing to say. As I had learned very young in life, if you have nothing good to say, say nothing. So I said nothing. I didn't get it. Mom was *not* a nice person; she was rude, crude and vindictive. Why would such a person be missed? I had to wonder if mom had some kind of dual personality. Was she one way with others and another way with her children? Or just different with me?

I had taken it upon myself to completely revamp the plans for mom's funeral. According to *her* wishes, her body would have been shipped to Las Vegas and there would be a huge mass there in her honor and she would be buried in a crypt next to my father. I wondered who would have attended that service. I knew that Ron and John would not go, so I decided to have the wake in Tennessee, a central location that would be easy for people to reach. Pauline and Jamie would not attend. Jamie had moved and had an unlisted phone number, so she was unreachable. I also knew, though, that she would not have cared about attending. She never forgave mom for putting her up for adoption (Fortunately, Jamie loved her adopted family and had a good life with them.) Pauline had dropped out of sight; she had earlier told me it was too difficult to be part of our family. After the funeral was over we would ship her body to Las Vegas and my mother would rest in a crypt next to my father.

Once it was all over, I stood there looking at the woman who gave me life. Well, at least I was grateful for that. Aware of tears running down my face, tears that I could not stop, I wondered why I was crying. My sadness was not for the woman, but for the *life* my mother and I did not have. I wondered what it would have been like to have a mother to turn to, to ask questions, a mother to hold me and tell me she loved me. A mother who would talk to me and tell me.

"Don't worry Joanne it'll all be okay." *That* was what I grieved for, longed for. I don't think that pain will ever heal, even with time.

When my mother passed away, my life did not change. Unlike other people who lose their mothers and say there is a void, I felt no void. It was almost as though she hadn't existed! My mother's behavior remains a study in confusion and frustration. She walked through life with a sense of entitlement, as though she had lived admirably. That always made me so angry, but I waited too long to tell her so. I have spent so long trying to convince myself that she didn't matter, that I was just fine without her, that she just didn't know how to be a mom, and on and on and on, but of course she did. As I watched her age and her health fail, I felt a sense of sadness for what might have been if circumstances had been otherwise and if she had been different. But it is irretrievable now. It helps me to look to the wisdom of these words from the singer Mary J. Blige:

"I blame my mother for nothing but I forgive her for everything." Perhaps that is the start of healing. Time will tell.

Fourteen

Not long after this we attended the funeral of my foster mother's daughter, Ada's husband Ray. Joe drove me to what used to be my foster home. We parked the car across the road and started walking toward the house when a car pulled in the driveway. A young girl got out.

"Do you live here?" I asked.

"Yes," she responded.

"I was raised in this house," I told her. Then this delightful young girl invited us in to take a look around. I had mixed feelings excitement and apprehension, since I was not sure how I would feel once I got inside.

Once inside I noticed how small everything seemed. As a child, the kitchen seemed very large and so did the dining room, with lots and lots of furniture. The new owners had changed the downstairs quite a bit, but pieces of it were still familiar. Then as we went upstairs, I noticed that they had removed the railing and changed the steps. It was then that I could not help but think, how many times had I climbed these stairs?

As I reached the top landing, memories came flooding back. Some were good, some bad but rushing back they came. I peeked inside the rooms that had housed our communal family. John's room and Emmeretta's room had been combined to make a master bedroom. Grandma's room was the same. As I entered the room that Gerry and I once shared, a room that seemed untouched in many ways, I was overcome with emotion. Tears began to flow… I knew it was a powerful moment. So much had happened in this house and I was in such a different life now. But in between the two lives, how many smaller lifetimes had transpired?

We went downstairs and out the back door to the yard. The young lady asked,

"Do you know why all these blue glass bottles were hidden all over the property? We found so many of them that we decided to put stakes along the driveway and put the bottles on them. We even named our home *Blue Bottle Farm*.

"Yes I do know," I said and then began to tell her the story about those blue bottles. She looked eager to hear it.

"When I lived here," I said,

"My foster father, whom we called Grandpa, used to go outside every night after dinner to enjoy a Bromo-Seltzer cocktail! He hid the bottles around the property because Grandma did not approve of this practice." The girl was amused and happy to have finally solved this mystery. She went to a shed where she kept the blue bottles and gave one to me as a keepsake. Now that bottle sits on my kitchen windowsill and every time I see it, I am transported back to the 1950's at least to the good memories of that time.

On our ride home I thanked Joe for his impulsive decision to drive by the house. I might not have done that on my own. How rich the results of that little excursion were!

Fifteen

I live a very different life now than the one I used to live. My life's journey has seen me through the poverty of a street kid, the foster care system, an abusive marriage and cancer. Once on my own I traveled my career path and then married the most wonderful man on the planet. I am wife, homemaker, mother, grandmother, sister and friend. I read to first graders and volunteered at SCORE (Senior Core of Retired Executives), and this life works for me. I have been enjoying the role of homemaker, cook for my family, and caretaker for our home. The kids know I am always available to help them and often I babysit those wonderful grandchildren. During this time, I have been able to reflect upon my life and marvel at this wonderful place of contentment I have come to. I cannot help but wonder how I got here. But as I retell my story, I see once again how it all happened. I believe that each one of us is in charge of getting to that place, if we make the choice and have a strong intention to do so.

I like to believe that I have taken all the negative things in my life and given them a positive spin. For me the tough times as a kid, helped me to survive as an adult. If life forces you to do the bad things in order to survive as a child, you can do really *good* things for others when you reach adulthood and help *them* to survive. With this awareness, we can try to not allow adverse circumstances to change our hearts and wound our spirits. And if by chance your heart is wounded or your spirit is diminished, each can be repaired. You can do it. You are what you choose to be. I had to believe this my whole life or I never would have moved forward at all.

In January, 2006, my husband hosted a sixty-third birthday party for me and invited friends and family who had been crucial in my life. As I looked around the room, I was overwhelmed with feelings of love and appreciation. Everyone there had been, at some time, good, bad or both involved in my life. They had always been there to support me. And those beautiful grandchildren, who renew my spirit daily and give my heart a reason to beat, were also there to help me celebrate.

At the time of this writing, my siblings are all doing well. Ron is married to his third wife, Terry. They are snow-birds living both in Long Island and Florida and are very happy. John is living in Georgia and at age sixty-two married Nancy on June 14, 2003. Gerry lives a half-hour from me with her husband Bob of forty-five years and they are both well and happy. Pauline is still somewhere in Alabama. We have lost touch, not because I want it that way, but because she chooses to stay out of touch. When Pauline contacted me after our reunion and told me it was too difficult to be a member of this family, I supported her feelings and told her I would always be there for her. A year or so later, Pauline had to have surgery. She was frightened and called me. I told her to get the surgery and that I would fly her to New York and nurse her back to health, which I did.

But some time later, when my stepdaughter Kerry was about to get married, I called Pauline to make flight arrangements for her. It was then she decided she would not attend the wedding. She said she had her own family and wanted to spend her vacation with them. I told her I totally understood but I never heard from her again. That was over ten years ago. Interestingly, she did call Gerry after the September 11th tragedy, knowing that Gerry's son, Robert, lived in Manhattan. Gerry explained her son was fine and thanked her for her concern. But she also never heard from Pauline again. Relationships require willingness on both sides, and unfortunately at this writing, my sister is not willing.

Jamie is living about a half hour away working and helping out with her grandchildren. Considering how fragmented we all were as a family, this amount of unity is quite remarkable.

But best of all, Joe and I are enjoying life and our family. We were fortunate enough to purchase a townhouse in Jupiter, Florida, where we spend the winter. We love to have our children and grandchildren fly down to spend time with us during their school breaks, and often remark how lucky we are to have this place. There is so much joy to be had when family and friends visit. As I watch my grandchildren frolic in the ocean my thoughts drift back to my childhood. I marvel at the life they have and the life I have made for myself. I never forget how lucky I am to have what I have. I never forget the people along the way who were willing to lend me a hand. I worked through the adversities in my life and tried to learn from them. I always tell my grandchildren, you can be anything you want to be. Just don't every give up on your dreams. You get one shot at life and if you aim yourself in the right direction you can hit the target. And I hit the target!

Don't get me wrong, it is a lot of work but it is worth it. Joe and I choose to make every day a wonderful one. For this I am most grateful.

No Record Of The Jackson Children

In preparing to gather information for this book, I wanted to be certain I had all my facts correct. I called the Leake and Watts Children's Home and was passed around from voicemail to voicemail. Finally I got the president's voicemail, James Campbell, and left a message. I also left a message for his secretary though I never heard from either of them. After contacting the archives office, I was told that there was no record of the Jackson children. No record of my siblings or me. None.

You can imagine my anger and frustration. My whole life I have felt invisible. Now it was confirmed that we did not exist at least on paper. I had visited Leake and Watts Children's Home and visited with the last social worker of record, Helen Auerbach, she handed me a piece of paper with abbreviated notes that indicated when we were removed from my mother's home, the year we were placed in a permanent foster home, when John and Pauline joined us in our foster home and when our faster father died. She got that information somewhere. I don't think she kept it in her memory for fifty-six years.

I find it extremely distressing that they were unwilling to assist me. Both my sister Gerry and I have received over the years, requests for contributions from Leake and Watts Children's Home. It seems odd to me that an organization which prides itself in helping children was unwilling to take the time to locate the information I requested for this project. As a result I have approximated some dates and ages.